Is This Book for Me?

If you are someone who wants to be in control of your life, if you want to be the captain of your ship, if you're tired of being a victim of circumstance, whether that be past, present or future, and you're motivated to become the conscious creator of your reality, this is for you. If you want to learn exactly what you can do to reduce and eliminate anxiety, panic attacks, depression, PTSD, OCD, insomnia, triggers, personality limitations, fibromyalgia and plenty more, this is your path. If you want to work to create a happier, calmer, more decisive, confident, pleasant, more energized and all-around better version of yourself, you have the power inside of you, and this book is your journey. I am your guide. Let's create a massively positive ripple effect in your life!

Purpose

I wrote this book to show others exactly how I beat my diagnoses, how I found purpose and meaning in the struggles of my past, and how I created a version of myself that could go onto help hundreds of millions of others. This is only the beginning. I am here to leave this world slightly better than it was when I entered it. I believe that we all have limitless potential within us, and that a happier, safer, stronger and more unified world is within our grasp. I believe that it starts with you.

-Khail

Waking Up from Anxiety
© 2019 Khail Kapp; Kapp Strategies LLC

Table of Contents

How to Change the World

"I am of the opinion that my life belongs to the whole community, and as long as I live it is my privilege to do for it whatever I can. I want to be thoroughly used up when I die, for the harder I work the more I live. I rejoice in life for its own sake. Life is no 'brief candle' for me. It is a sort of splendid torch which I have got hold of for the moment, and I want to make it burn as brightly as possible before handing it on to future generations."
-George Bernard Shaw

I chose this path. I never thought it would get this hard, but it was my responsibility from the start. As I sit in my car underneath breathtaking (or are they breath-giving?) sequoia trees just outside "The trail of 100 Giants" in California, I am miles away from another human and 50 miles away from cell phone reception. I am obsessed. I believe very deeply that I will see drastic change towards world peace in my lifetime, and I believe I am to play a major role. I have this burning desire to help people and thankfully, I am really good at it. I'm lying in my car finishing up this book, a project in the works for over a year now. I am beyond excited to know that you're reading this, because it is going to change your life.

I hated the name "Khail" (sounds like kale) when I was young. Growing up, it rhymed with too many things and I hated the woman that gave me the name. But it has a meaning that I've finally lived up to. Khail means "friend to all".

When I started coaching, my plan was simply to show people how to be more present, how to improve their lives and relationships, and ultimately, how to be happier. But it wasn't until I started talking about anxiety that I was able to make huge, transformational impacts on people's lives.

Months before I began, I had hit rock bottom. Growing up in an abusive household, PTSD, insomnia, and depression were things I was "managing". I had always been anxious and neurotic, but I started to spiral out of control and everything changed.

My wife and I were disagreeing too often, which escalated to fighting, which transformed into a choreographed play and we would both simultaneously switch to angry-autopilot. The mind's program was at work, but the settings were all screwed up.

In a freak gym accident, I tore my pec muscle in a unique way, at the musculotendinous junction. Rather than snapping the tendon, something easily repaired in under an hour (Side note: I was a medical device representative for years, consulting products that would fix tendons and fractures), I managed to peel most of the muscle belly away from the tendon. My pec was hanging on by a thread. Let's just say my little brother's first impression of the gym could've been smoother. I'm getting somewhere with this.

For 2 weeks I could hardly move my arm away from my body, and had my hand tucked into my armpit like a T-Rex or horrible bird impression. I started to become triggered into states of panic when I would look at my son, fearing I would have to jolt my arm to catch him. Not an unreasonable concern for a parent with a young, kamikaze toddler. I would lock myself away in the bedroom and cry while trying to calm down. I finally had everything I wanted in life, but panic and anxiety were robbing my entire experience.

I was already having panic attacks on the freeway while driving with my family, not sleeping, our marriage was suffering, my medical device career was spiraling, and now I was prescribed a CPAP machine for "moderately severe sleep apnea".

One night I couldn't take it anymore. In an ugly cry with my face down in the carpet, I realized that I had always been right. I'd won every argument, easily achieved good grades, always felt like the smartest guy in the room, outshined my fellow coworkers at nearly every task, and I was a master at researching. But I was miserable. It didn't matter how much money I was making, where I lived, how many friends or plans I'd have, how deep my research got, or even how far away from the abusive environment I grew up in. I would always wind up finding myself in the same situations. The same relationships, the same job drama, the same family arguments. I realized there was only one thing that was the same everywhere I went. Me.

I may have grown and learned, but I hadn't mastered this particular problem yet. I thought that it must all be related. I realized that I didn't want to be right anymore. I didn't want to be this old version of Khail. I didn't care what it took. At times I would ponder a lobotomy. But I wanted to figure it out. I wanted growth.

Whatever it took, I wanted to be happy.

That was the recipe. Choosing happiness and growth over everything. That was how it started. But it grew into something so much more. As I changed my mindset, everything changed. I quit everything else and focused on researching happiness, consciousness, going back through my notes from college (Pre-Medicine: majoring in biology with a minor in psychology), religious texts, philosophy, physiology and those basics of quantum physics we nerds love to try to wrap our heads around.

I started looking at the world like a game. A game where everything was happening FOR me, rather than TO me. Everything was there to teach me a lesson. But this sleep apnea had to go. I will later describe to you what worked for me. Please be responsible and consult a doctor before doing anything silly.

I realized while feeling lightheaded every time I would stand up, due to anxiety, that I would also feel winded easily. Part of that I could tell was because it seemed like I was always holding my breath. This led to tension, even physical pain and more anxiety. But I also would notice that I was easily winded doing menial tasks and my breathing felt weaker.

I decided to research deep belly breathing techniques and I mastered what I like to call, the "Pause Breath", explained later in this book. This breathing technique helped me reduce all physical symptoms of anxiety, completely cured my sleep apnea and any use for a CPAP, and eliminated my panic attacks. The rest of what I teach helps eliminate the physical symptoms and rewire the mind for calm. This program will not only help you develop the skills to eliminate the negative, it will send you on a limitless path of growth! I no longer suffer from any diagnoses mentioned, or any not mentioned. I no longer suffer.

Once I started feeling better, my world opened up. I had more time, more energy, more love. I felt like I was unfolding, and I wanted to share this warmth with the world. After posting several videos about how to be happier, I started getting vulnerable about my past and the triumphs I've had with mental illnesses. This is what brought people to me. When people started asking for help with anxiety, I found a clear path to teach people how to live without suffering. So, I made a deal.

Call it God, the Universe, Source, energy, consciousness, awareness or rationality. It doesn't matter what you call it, but I made a deal with it all and said that if our bills were paid for the next 2 months, I would devote my life to helping others live. I naively thought that 2 months was all the time I needed to build a business that helps people and supports my family.

I should've made a better deal.

Some unexpected fortunes, a surgeon booked a few cases with my product out of the blue, and our bills were covered for exactly two months. It was magic. It was a sign (the first of countless). So, I continued to help anyone that would listen, collecting stories of chaos turned clear, fear turned to love, families mending wounds and people finding purpose! 7 months later we packed about 20% of our belongings into storage, 10% fit into cars along with our two children and 2 dogs, and we gave the rest to charity and a few neighbors. It felt good to minimize.

I was helping hundreds of people through emails, voice messaging and texting, 1-on-1 calls and group coaching. My past and passion gave me purpose. People were leaving the house for the first time in 20 years by themselves. Marriages were being rekindled. Parents were completely changing the trajectory of the relationships with their children. PTSD, ADHD, Pure-O OCD, Fibromyalgia, Insomnia, constant Anxiety symptoms and Panic Attacks were vanishing all around me. I helped several decide not to commit suicide. Best of all, I realized a higher calling for myself.

I saw that people were suffering beyond measure, some on the brink of death or suicide, some hurting the very things they hold most dear, **but most of all I saw so many scared souls who were fooled into believing they'd been broken.**

I could hardly create a business out of this. Selling a product that removes fear to people that think through a filter of fear revealed itself to be quite challenging. Scared people don't typically like new things. I wanted to give up. Honestly, I've thought many, many times about throwing away my gift to transform people's lives and getting some random job. Poverty, stress, and begging people to try to work for their happiness grew old at times. To be transparent, I actually did decide to get a job and interviewed with 3 companies. I made it through weeks of each company's interview process only to find myself feeling very out of place during the last interviews. It was supernatural. I was a shoo-in, had recommendations and friends in the company, the most experience and great skills for the jobs. But somehow it was like we were speaking different languages in the last interviews. It was like I was forced to keep my promise to focus on helping people.

I was in the belly of the whale. Life grew more challenging. Three months into couch surfing with the family and dogs, and I still hadn't created a business that stuck. My wife and children moved in with her parents for many good reasons, such as better quality of life and more help for my toddlers, but also for a few important reasons I'll mention. This decision to help people was rough on our marriage and both of us needed to grow if we were going to prioritize helping others above everything. We needed to redefine our relationship.

My aunt and godmother, Trish, was absolutely incredible in helping us for months! My children were blessed to have her presence. While I filmed my course in the library at Penn State, my alma mater, my wife and retired aunt would create engaging activities for the family. Trish was the person who recommended I fill this book with inspiring testimonials, so much of the credit for this work needs to go to her for that great idea!

My mother and step father took us in for months as well, buying us groceries and accommodating our entire clan so wonderfully. My in-laws have helped in more ways than I am able to list, and I will be forever humbled by their giant hearts. And for nearly a year my father bankrolled my coaching business, helping us pay for so many bills.

(Honestly, realistically, there are a million people to thank. So many helped me along my way both directly and indirectly. To thank them all, I've worked hard to bring this work to you in a format that can help you transform your entire life.)

I reaffirmed my choice to help people no matter how bleak the circumstances got. I believe that helping someone live is more important than anything. To me, saving a life is more important than any desire I have. I also believe that I can always meet my basic needs, so if I am breathing, I am helping.

It is amazing how everything comes together in life. I often say that we don't always get what we want but we always have everything we need.

5 months into couch surfing and living out of a backpack, and it was time for change. I went to live in my car. Pennsylvania gets pretty cold in the winter and I'd always wanted to move back to California. My wife and I agreed that I should travel (based on a million factors including how we would redefine our relationship and grow closer, spiritual signs, and where the business seemed to be leading us).

Now as I write this, I have been living in my car for just about 3 months. It has been a wild ride. As I've lived off cans of chicken and veggies, bathed in the ocean and worked 12+ hour days in coffee shops, lost 20 pounds and nearly run out of gas without a penny to my name on a few occasions, all while being thousands of miles from my babies (my choice, and I GET TO cultivate a rich relationship with them once I land on my feet), I still continued to inspire, coach and help transform the lives of many. I think it gives me a little credit. I'm the homeless hero. An anxiety coach who's comfortable living in his car has to count for something, right? I hadn't made a big deal about living in my car because to me, it isn't.

It takes some getting used to, and trust me, I could write a book on the downsides. But **I don't write my stories like that.** I'm grateful. I've learned more about myself and life in the past few months than I've learned in the 32 years leading up to this moment.

To the people that challenged me, hated me, and believed in me, thank you for your lessons. If you have decided to read this book in hopes of getting better, I know it will help you, and even if it only helps just you and just a little, it was worth everything I have gone through.

Life is a journey. Sometimes we need to trust we are on the right path. Keep moving but enjoy the walk.

Introduction

"My crown is in my heart, not in my head; not decked with diamonds,
nor to be seen.
My crown is called content, a crown that seldom kings enjoy."
-William Shakespeare

Congratulations on having the courage to change and the willingness to try. It means the world to me knowing that you are reading this. A happier you means a better world for me too. Keep your willingness to do the right thing for yourself and continue to feed into your courage to change!

Congratulations on investing in yourself. It is important that we start here: congratulating you. You need to start focusing more on you. You need to take better care of yourself and that is what this book is all about. Self-love. Afterall, this is the core of essentially every problem. I'll explain more about what that means later.

To start, imagine yourself as the parent on a crashing plane. You must apply your oxygen mask first before attempting to help anyone else, otherwise you may fail to help anyone properly. Now, if you don't have a new journal or notebook to keep track of your thoughts as you embark on this journey, get one!

Understand that a better version of you will have a positive ripple effect on everyone. Your conversations, encouragements and judgments, reactions, sense of creativity and presence will all be improved by this mindset.

Know that the greatest gift you can give the world is your well-being.

So, congratulations on investing in your family, in your coworkers, your friends and literally every single person you will ever come into contact with.

I am determined to create a positive ripple effect around the world, and that starts with real transformations from people like you. By applying the wisdom you will gather from studying this book, you'll become "more". More loving, patient or calmer, and that version of you will be "better" to the entire world.

You may not like everything I am going to tell you. You may not like my writing style or the order of the chapters I've decided on (all purposeful I assure you). **Your mind will do everything it can to try find something wrong,** because it will stop at nothing to keep you exactly where you are. Safe. Reliable. I would etch this into your understanding now the best that you can. Your mind will try to trick you this way for the rest of your life.

The mind is comfortable right now because it is surviving. It doesn't care if you are anxious, depressed or even on the verge of suicide. Right now, it is surviving. It wants your personality, your pet-peeves, your triggers and fears to remain exactly where they are, or worse, it would prefer that they box you in even tighter because that looks "safe" to the mind.

So, it is up to you! It is up to you to ignore the discomfort and digest everything that you can. Squeeze every bit of value from this material and I promise you that your life will never be the same!

You've got to stay committed. We are going to start with laying a foundation for strength and calmness in your life. The practices you must commit to may seem tedious or difficult, but if you stay consistent, I promise you that they'll become fun and you will completely transform your life for the better!

There's nothing I can do right now to force you to follow what I teach. But understand that if you can't commit to laying the right foundation, you will never build a sturdy place to live. My methods are to help cure you forever, to show you how to be resilient against any obstacle that comes your way. This isn't about a temporary fix. This isn't a pill. And if you take everything sincerely from here on out, learning to flow with life, you will do much more than just cure your illness. You will evolve into an optimized version of yourself and see a clear path to overcome any obstacles in your way.

Imagine that for a moment. What are you trying to change in your life? What will you do with all the time you used to spend worrying? What will that new version of yourself look like? Take a moment and jot down how your voice sounds, the facial expression and look in your eyes, and anything around you that might represent this new version of yourself. We will be diving into this deeper in later chapters, but for now write down a few points and simply ponder on them for a moment before continuing.

My "WHY"

_____

_____

_____

_____

_____

_____

_____

_____

_____

_____

_____

_____

_____

_____

_____

_____

_____

_____

_____

_____

_____

_____

_____

_____

Now, go back through this list and describe what this will mean for others in your life. How will your relationships improve? Describe what will change for the better, where you will go (travel, career, etc.), and how life could unfold. **This is your why** and it will be something you will want to come back to, sharpen and redefine as time goes on.

You've taken this first step towards betterment. You CAN do this! You WILL do this. Just stay committed and follow through. I can't stress this enough. Write this down: "I am committed". Put this somewhere you can reflect on every single day over the next 6 weeks or more. Clients that get the best from my work have a single notebook for their growth. So along with this workbook, have a separate and exclusive place to keep notes and journal any and all things related to your new journey. Know that this is a process and will take time.

Whatever it takes. No matter how hard life gets, no matter how many times you fall off the horse, you must always get back on.
It doesn't matter when, as long as you do it.

I've designed a group to help you stay motivated along this journey. Join here:
https://facebook.com/groups/khail.kapp/
Be a member. Socialize. Let's grow together!

I've read many books and paid for a ton of courses on self-improvement. To let you know a little bit more about myself, I don't like fluff. I want answers that I can apply to my life and grow in the most efficient way possible.

Know that if it is in this book, it is important for your life. Make sure you take notes, keep a journal, set goals and stay committed. Read through the chapters as many times as it takes to understand how each lesson applies to your life. This book builds off of itself and gets more complex as you read. Go slowly. Life is not a race. Keep in mind that you want to *calm* your anxiety.

Above everything, be kind to yourself and don't take life too seriously.

Would you like a **FREE CHEATSHEET** to compliment this book? It's yours! Follow the link below! This sheet is well worth your time! Don't worry, I won't spam you.

https://khailkapp.com/cheat-sheet

Defining the Monster: Anxiety

"The primary cause of unhappiness is never the situation, but your thoughts about it."
-Eckhart Tolle

Anxiety is a disease caused by the longing for inspiration, presence and purpose, drowning in the flood of fear, need and distraction. It is the mind and body in a constant battle, living danger with the fear button stuck in the on position. It is the mastered practice of feeling dis-ease, angst, and discomfort.

It becomes ingrained in our being like roots in the earth. It pulls from every direction, fueling the body with everything negative, poisoning your very being to the core.

It is the mind's favorite multi-tool, and like an awful infomercial the mind starts using anxiety to cut through copper pipes and pick out groceries. Untouched, the mind will eventually use it for everything. Like a virus spreading into every aspect of life, infecting drive, love, closest relationships and every bit of happiness. It doesn't stop or drift away by itself. It becomes you.

Anxiety is a global pandemic resulting from people not knowing how to be human. Breathing, moving, learning how to be happy and managing our emotions would seem to me like practical first steps, yet billions of children are raised without these fundamentals. We have developed a culture that believes in time-travel: forever living in worry of the future and regret of the past. It is global, because it is nature's way of demanding change.

Pain promotes progress.

To give a practical perspective on anxiety before learning how to manage it and then eliminate it, let's rewind back thousands of years ago before modern technology, to a small village with our star character, Bob the caveman.

Bob is walking through the forest when he is attacked by a tiger. His subconscious mind signals "flight" to the body, which releases adrenaline and increases agility. Bob's perception for every little detail, especially with the intention of "exit", drastically heightens. Barely escaping with his life, he sprints back to the village.

Bob is instantly compelled to share his story with the other villagers. How did Bob survive this attack? Why did Bob tell his fellow villagers about the tiger? Simple. The brain and nervous system are wired for this. The body wants to live.

To ensure Bob's survival, the subconscious mind took care of the tricky work, and passed the breathing off to Bob at some point. Breathing is interesting that way. It is something you don't have to think about, until you do, and then you must.

Get what I mean? Think about breathing, and it becomes a conscious effort. And when we exercise or run, it often takes a bit of attention to breathe efficiently.

Begin to notice just how poor your breathing is when anxiety strikes.

Shallow, tense. Soon we will discuss how to correct it.

Back to Bob. The best thing to ensure the survival of the species is to spread the fear. Knowledge is power right? There are many clichés out there that disempower us, and this is one of them. Knowledge without action is often debilitating. We are wired to spread fearful knowledge.

There are many studies on the release of oxytocin when humans bond. Oxytocin is the beautiful chemical released when we bond, when a mother is breastfeeding her child, and when we hug. How do most conversations sound today? What are people connecting on? Problems. The weather. Our crappy bosses and jobs. Our fears and struggles. How many support groups for anxiety are you in? How many couches have you laid back on to vent? What percentage of your conversations are made up of complaining, judging or fearing?

Don't feel bad. It is only natural. We are compelled to do this because it feels right. And it *feels* right because we become slaves to our limbic systems, rationalizing our feelings without question. Without being mindful enough to separate yourself from your feelings, reacting to them and through them becomes habit. But this program will teach you to kick that habit and create many helpful new habits.

Anxiety is like an ancient tool for survival that just goes haywire with anything negative. When you feel like complaining or venting, know that this is your primitive mind talking. Some things need to be said like "hey your kitchen is on fire", but those things have an actionable step. Overall, most complaints and negativity are just filling the silence. We are compelled to blurt out what's wrong and what we don't like about things.

When you are being overwhelmed by symptoms, know that the body is just confused. It is just the fight or flight response. You may have heard of a 3rd party called the "freeze" response that was recently added. I don't believe in this. We would not have made it this far as a species if the freeze response was a natural reaction for us. We freeze now because fighting is dangerous or completely uncalled for and running whenever we feel anxious would be awkward to say the least.

Much of today's anxiety is a result of the fear of being socially awkward.

Imagine people racing past your car every time there was a traffic jam or doing laps in a conference room during a business meeting. Imagine punching a random cashier square in the face because you felt anxious trying to dig the credit card out of your wallet.

Our society has not set us up to release the adrenaline rush felt at so many inappropriate times like when a police officer pulls up behind you despite your perfect and law-abiding conditions, or when the volume on a loud-speaker is set just a little too loud and an announcement takes you off guard. No, our society is designed around comfort and ease. And our ancient bodies still believe that anything that doesn't feel good is probably danger. If our choices don't pan out or life throws us a curve ball, BAM, the body starts to feel anxious.

Constant adrenaline releases aren't the body's favorite experience to simply sit through. Your heart pumps frantically to channel those fight or flight chemicals to muscles that could use them, and the muscles don't. So, now you become shaky with an increased heartrate.

Your adrenaline-fueled mind races to notice every minute detail, and rather than look for ways to defend against a tiger attack, your eyes dart to exits, attention focuses on bodily functions and multi-tasking worry, and bottled up excitement turns to fear. This fear creates perpetual loops of negative "intrusive thinking" that replay again and again, empowering the fear, adding emotional weight to it, and making it so "real".

Where you would normally be breathing deeply in the middle of fighting to fleeing, you're sitting still, breathing shallow or holding your breath, and keeping your body tense. Your mind gets foggy and you become dizzy due to lack of oxygen.

Hyperventilation doesn't give your lungs enough time to absorb oxygen and you feel like you're going to pass out.

Remember the perception increase, where ancient Bob could see all around the forest? Well, now you're looking for every exit, noticing every detail, every movement. You imagine that the man behind the register or woman 3 spots behind you are judging everything about you. You can feel their breaths and sense their frustration. Every movement seen out of the corner of your eye confirms that you are holding them up. The mind works to help you prove what you believe, and I will talk about that more in the next section.

This ancient technology might seem like it is against you. That is simply because parts of it seem mysterious or off-limits to you right now. But this is your body, your technology to master, your path to walk.

Mind of Its Own

"If you correct the mind, the rest of your life will fall into place."
-Lao Tzu

For thousands of years the brain has hardly changed. In fact, it has gotten about 10% smaller, which really can't be good for our mental health in today's technology driven world.

Comparing us to cavemen may seem like apples and oranges. To give you a better perspective on the survival machine you're operating, 150 years ago wolves were a common problem for people in the United States. Wolves would jump through window openings and gobble up families in a time that wasn't far from now and not too many generations ago. How far detached from a survival mindset could we possibly be?

Lucky for us, changing the software changes the hardware. Change *the way* you think, and you will begin to believe and behave in a manner that suits your new perspective.

The mind can be looked at as the software to the brain's hardware, and both can be dramatically upgraded. I believe that we can upgrade to levels we cannot even fathom. That is how awareness works. The more consciously aware you are, the deeper, more colorful and captivating everything becomes. Things you once knew, you now know on a deeper level. This is what's referred to as "waking up". I digress.

First, the brain is an absorption machine. It only takes IN information. No delete button up there. This means that everything you expose yourself to: the music you listen to, the shows you binge watch, the movies you see, the books you read, the conversations, fights, and arguments you have, even the thoughts you think and the words you say are all being hardwired into your mind. Deeper still are the feelings that each bit of data elicits in your body. This all weighs heavily on HOW you experience the world and your overall state-of-being.

Just what are you exposing yourself to? List some of the things below that may actually encourage and instigate your struggles. Some examples are the news, Dr. Google, a poor relationship, support groups that are filled with fear and worry, **the way you view** triggers and certain times of the day or month. Once you've written these out, make a conscious effort to limit or even eliminate these anxiety-encouraging behaviors.

My Anxiety Fuel

_____

_____

_____

_____

_____

_____

_____

The mind is wired for survival, which can be the same as saying it's wired for negativity. Allow me to elaborate this perspective.

We are wired to seek out everything and anything that is wrong with the world around us. We're always trying to optimize. It is why we have a new version of the same phone every year that is just slightly better than the last. It is why technology grows exponentially, and it is why we are living in the most depressed and anxious time in human history, yet at the same time, it is the safest time in history to be a human. Fun facts.

The mind is not wired for inner-peace. Imagine, thousands of years ago, being grateful for everything, whistling through the jungle with a big goofy smile on your face. You may as well have doused yourself in steak sauce and imitated lion mating calls.

Fortunately, there's neuroplasticity. This is the mind's ability to change PHYSICAL SHAPE. Not just teaching an old dog new tricks. Not only changing the chemicals in our heads, but actual physical shape of the brain! This is your hard wiring for belief. Neuroplasticity means your ability to change who you are down to the very core.

One of my favorite studies is from Harvard, and it describes the amazing positive effects of breathing and mindfulness practices on traumatic football injuries. Subjects repaired physical brain damage with the right thoughts and practices! Do you believe that your anxiety is worse than traumatic brain damage caused by a 250lb linebacker? Don't try to answer that just yet. As you continue to digest this information, you will prove to yourself just how powerful you and your mind are.

I am not going to fill this book with statistics, studies and references. The internet is a plethora of knowledge. Feel free to research anything the NIH posts and specifically for this point, Dr. Daniel G. Amen. I know. How taboo to not fill my book with references to prove to you how much science I know.

To sum up the first point: **stop talking about anxiety**! Talking about anxiety is just hardwiring your subconscious mind to experience more of it. Don't complain about it. Leave the support groups that only ever talk about their fears, medications and horrible experiences, as these will only promote and enable you to experience more of what you don't want.

That's right. Like some kind of underground fighting group, the folks who get better using Khail's methods have to stick to rule #1: no more talking about anxiety.

Your friends and relatives may not understand your struggle. Good. That is just a few less people you will have to convince that you're changing and growing while you're working on yourself. You may have an entire list of people you call every time things get stressful. Change the subject with them. Start talking about the experience you actually wish to have, rather than the experience that you do not. This is incredibly hard for people to wrap their heads around so I will say it again. Start talking about the experience you actually wish to have, rather than the experience you are trying to get away from.

Write down 3 of the things you actually want while avoiding mentioning anxiety. So instead of writing "be free from anxiety", write "enjoy the freedom and excitement of driving wherever/whenever I want".

_____

_____

_____

_____

_____

_____

To sum up the second point, our minds and our upbringing may have set the stage for us to think with fear, stress and anxiety, but the mind is the most powerful tool in the universe, and it can be wired for any experience.

> *"For over 20 years I had suffered with anxiety and panic attacks. Grocery stores, driving, and simply being alone with my children brought me panic. I was amazed at just how much rewiring and change could occur using my mind. Within a week of Khail's program I was 50% better! Within 2 months I was driving on the freeway again (hadn't done that in 7 years)! I now know I will live a life FREE and not a victim of anxiety. Khail is truly a special and gifted human. He is meant to heal people. I can't recommend him enough."*
> **-Sandy Fleming**

Stop Practicing Anxiety

"He who fights with monsters should be careful lest he thereby become a monster. And if thou gaze long into an abyss, the abyss will also gaze into thee."
-Friedrich Nietzsche

The mind is constantly optimizing. Constantly trying to make our lives easier and more efficient. These words sound positive, right? Efficiency! Ease! Optimization! Wow, these must be positive...

Well, not necessarily. You could more easily catch a cold if your immune system is weak. You can efficiently fall down a flight of steps if we grease the railing and staircase just right. Your life, your body and mind can be completely optimized for anxiety and panic attacks if you're practicing them enough. Chances are, your body and mind are. `

How? If you have them often, you're practicing them. What percentage of your life are you devoting to worry? How much time do you spend thinking or talking about anxiety? You can fear more easily if you are feeding into your fears, talking about them, googling, deeply submerging yourself into support groups. Desensitization doesn't always take place, and fear easily becomes an addiction.

Now, let's slow down. Hear me. You are getting very good at being distracted by distracting yourself often. With your phone, checking your social media and your emails, constantly messaging, constantly scrolling. By filling the silence with chatter, filling the stillness with random thought, you are in NEED of distraction.

You might be a seasoned veteran at beating yourself up. Constantly talking down to yourself, allowing your head to be filled with worry and doubt. Have you practiced this method since you were a child?

You're not a bad person. All that is revealed should simply be seen as "ah-hah moments" for you to capitalize on.

See beating anxiety has so much to do with not practicing anxious behaviors. Not constantly distracting yourself. Not NEEDING your phone or some kind of noise to fill the peacefully silent present. Not NEEDING to have things a certain way. Beating anxiety is about cutting off all the negative fuel sources.

What does anxiety feel like? Think about this for a second. NEED. Tight grip. Fear. Negativity. Avoidance. Doubt. Feelings of lack. Guilt. Worry and embarrassment.

You must analyze your life and look for negative and anxious behaviors and try to practice these less. And while you're at it, continue to practice a calmer lifestyle. There are calmer ways to do the tasks you are currently doing with angst and frustration. In the next sections you will learn exactly how to interrupt these harmful patterns and wire yourself for peace!

> "Khail Kapp has changed my life! He gave me the strength, tools and confidence for me to change myself from the inside out. Inner peace is what I seek every day! I suffered from depression, anxiety, and PTSD... NO MORE! It starts with me, I am in CONTROL of my OWN HAPPINESS. No one else. I control what I can and the rest I let go. There are no words to describe my gratitude!"
> **-Amie Mignogna**

Laying the Foundation

The minute you settle for less than you deserve,
you get less than you settled for.

The techniques and routines described in this section may seem too simple. They may also seem irrelevant. Again, I assure you that this program has no fluff and that **everything I teach has a purpose and is important for you.**

I can't stress enough how necessary these are in training your body for calm and eliminating anxiety in your life. You don't have to trust me, but why not test me? Why not use that inner-skeptic to prove, without a shadow of a doubt, that you know whether or not my program will work for you? Now we are talking. Stay committed and I will give you some tricks to help keep you motivated along the way.

Take out the notebook. By this time you ought to have something else to write in, so go ahead and fetch that amazing notebook. This notebook along with my workbook will be a testament to the massive change you will experience over the next few weeks.

Would you like to learn the first minor lifestyle change that will dramatically improve your mood, wellness, sleep, your overall state of being, and if you're a lady: your periods or the transition of menopause? This magical tip I am going to share with you will help you live longer and happier, make you smarter and stronger, and guess what, you have access to it right now. What is it?

It's water. I'm not kidding. Most likely, right now, you don't drink remotely enough water, but that must stop. You need to drink a minimum of 100oz of water every day.

Google it. The requirements we learned as kids were wrong. We need roughly 100oz.

So, go measure whatever you drink out of right now. Seriously! Stop everything for a moment. I know how it feels to want to continue reading, but this is a workbook as much as it is full of lessons, and that urge to do it your way needs to be calmed if you are going to learn to do things my way. Think about it. Has your way been working?

Ready? Let's get to work! Figure out what 100oz looks like and make a commitment right now to drink enough every single day. If you drink out of the same cup, measure that, and count how many of those cups you need until you reach 100oz.

No, soda and juice do not count as water. Soda, coffee and beer are taking away from your water supply. Anything with caffeine such as certain teas and anything with alcohol is subtracting from the water you drink.

You might not be a fan of water, but you will be once you start drinking it more regularly. Your body is going to encourage you to drink more once you get used to it, because frankly, your body really enjoys being hydrated. Try squirting a little lemon or cranberry juice in water to add flavor. I did this for years. I was raised on juice and now I never buy it. I carry around stainless steel water bottles wherever I go.

If you don't like peeing as much as this is going to make you pee, question: do you hate panic attacks more than peeing? Do you hate getting sick, feeling weak or dizzy, or being more irritable, mor than peeing? Get comfy on that toilet as your body starts to function in a cleansing, detoxifying way like never before.

If you crave fruit or something sweet, drink a cup of water first. Chances are you really don't need the sugar and you are probably just thirsty. I've found that most of the time I or my clients want something sweet, it's really dehydration coming on.

Drink the water! You WILL thank me! You may find it hard to build up to this much hydration. Try drinking first thing in the morning. If you start your day with coffee, have a nice helping of water first and wait a half hour. You'll be astonished at what hydration will do for your energy levels! In fact, when I have feelings of lethargy throughout the day, most of the time it is simply because I am a little dehydrated.

Lastly, there are a few recommendations I do have if you are interested in supplements. These aren't necessary, but I know they can help. Organic fish-oil, magnesium, calcium, and vitamin D are all very helpful for happiness and the mind. Avoiding booze, caffeine, sugar and fried foods, or at least limiting them along this journey will be helpful as well. My teachings are to keep with you wherever you go. On a bus, on a train, in a box with a fox. So, if you're interested in diet and exercise, that is great, and I encourage it, but this program will essentially focus on what you have at your disposal 24/7.

You may have certain triggers that are within your control to avoid. While you are learning the lessons and building a foundation for calm, it is best to avoid what you can, and anything that you can't change, try not to take too seriously.

Right now, I drink _____oz of water on a good day. My typical drinking cup/bottle carries _____oz, so I will drink _____ (how many) daily.

The Pause Breath

When you breathe into something, you in-spire, giving it life.

You may have tried breathing exercises before. I want you to forget what you know and give mine a shot for the next **4 weeks minimum** before you decide to give up.

This is like learning an instrument or a new sport. It is going to be rough sometimes. One day you might think you've got it down and the next day it might not have the same effect. This routine may seem too simple to have an effect, but I assure you it is pertinent. Stick with it. You WILL master it.

I've seen people notice symptoms dissipate and even vanish within the first week by only committing to the breathing technique. It is powerful!

The trick to mastering my breathing technique as fast as possible is to set an alarm. Set the timer on your phone for a minimum of every hour. Every time that timer goes off, click repeat, stop what you're doing, and dive into your Pause Breath.

People ask, "how many times should I practice every time my alarm goes off?" Easy. Does it feel good? If yes, do you really want to stop feeling good and get back to feeling like crap? You might as well do it a few times. If it doesn't feel great yet, perhaps doing it a few times will help? See what I mean? The work you put in equates to what you get out.

Push yourself to do more every day, and you will be more, any day.

Ask yourself, "how often do I actually put myself into a calm state." How often do you use your mind to get calm? Not how often your environment, dog, phone, meds, or anything else outside of you makes you feel calm, but how often you are responsible for this using your very own will-power?

The more you train to calm yourself, the easier it will get, despite your environment! You want to develop calm like a reflex, so that eventually you can stop panic before it starts. But for now, train while its easy and train frequently. Are you taking notes on the mindset behind this? Do it!

"Do it now!"
-Arnold Schwarzenegger

Ok, that was a silly one. We take life too seriously, so that isn't fluff. Keep things fun.

Another common question people ask is, "how many times a day should I do this?" Same answer. As many as you can and want to commit to! Every hour is my minimum recommendation, but I've worked with clients who set their alarm every 15 minutes and notice very rapid healing. You will be blown away at how often this alert will catch you in the middle of a negative thought. It will be magical.

Note: Quality is more important than quantity here, and I will get to that.

If you're busy, you're driving or working, if you are mid conversation with someone and the timer goes off, no problem. Either get yourself to a quiet and calm place like the bathroom or pull the car over, or simply practice this exercise with your eyes wide open. If you miss an alert or forget to reset, make it up to yourself when you catch a break.

Why have breathing exercises failed you in the past? Have you practiced one this rigorously before? Unlikely. I love you, but let's be honest here. Most likely you've only practiced breathing when you wanted panic to go away. Even if you've tried a breathing technique for weeks like this, the method behind mine will still prove helpful!

Ultimately, know that if you practice this when it is easiest to practice, when you are in a quiet and comfortable place, completely undisturbed, you will master it faster.

Before I teach you exactly how to do the Pause Breath, I want you to come up with a purely positive story. This can be a memory, a description of a child or a pet, or even a food or restaurant that you love. The goal here with this story is to be <u>extremely specific</u>, peeling back the layers and immersing yourself, getting lost for a moment, keeping it completely positive, and <u>eliciting a good feeling</u>.

So, if you describe your wedding day, you may write that it was beautiful even though your mother in law did something bad. It was perfect, but it did rain and you were nervous. This can't work. It might be tricky for you to do this because it goes against our human nature to focus purely on positive. I had such a hard time thinking positively that I resorted to a box of kittens. I had everything I ever wanted in life and I couldn't even get myself to feel good. You're not alone.

For weeks I thought about a box of kittens for more than 10 times per day.

The next point about this story is that it must be very specific to one thing or event, not a bunch of childhood memories, but one very specific thing. Connect as many senses as you can to this story or idea. I could write: my dog, Kita, has that new puppy smell. I love her vibrant brindle fur, all different shades of browns and black. Her big silly ears point off her head like wings on a bat. She always smiles and smiles even greater when I look at her and call her towards me. She is relentlessly loving, and I can get lost in her deep, orangey eyes.

And like that I get completely lost in positivity. I manage to turn my thoughts into feelings. Now we are talking the body's language.

Feeling is the language of the body and brain.

Take a pause from reading and write your story below. Make it a nice sized paragraph, purely positive and very detailed. Peel back the layers. The goal is to feel it!

My Purely Positive Story (Game Changer)

_____

_____

_____

_____

_____

_____

_____

_____

_____

_____

The next most important way for me to write is to **pull your eyes** to this sentence so that I can say, "hey, what do you think you're doing? Write that positive story before moving on! This is for YOU! I want you well! Write that story! This isn't my first rodeo, partner! I've helped people with anxiety for a long time and that need to find your answers in 'the next thing' needs to be calmed. Play along. It is for your own good." - Khail

I was prescribed a CPAP machine to help me breathe after committing to several sleep studies and being diagnosed with moderately severe sleep apnea (the second worst type). Mastering this technique alone completely cured my sleep apnea. It has helped hundreds cure their anxiety and even more cure their insomnia. And it is going to help bring you into the present moment, train your body to feel calm as easily as a reflex, and you will tip the scales of your mind towards more positivity in your life. It will help you gain control over your emotions and it will be the tool you use to change everything you don't like about your life.

The following is incredibly detailed. Highlight, take notes, make bullets, and above everything keep coming back to make sure you have it understood! This technique is your key to everything else, so take it sincerely!

To perform this breathing technique, get somewhere calm and quiet as often as possible. Sit up, spine erected, shoulders back and chin up. Lay your hands on your knees with your palms up. Close your eyes. Slowly inhale through your nose, **paying very close attention to the feeling of the air** as it enters your nostrils. Listen to the sound. Allow your belly to expand while you are inhaling. This may feel strange to you at first. You may want to put your hand on your chest to allow your belly to come out while you are inhaling. You may also want to try this while lying down until you master belly breathing.

You must attempt to focus all your attention on the breathing, the stretching of your belly, the tickling of the air in your nostrils, etc. Breathe very slowly and deeply for about 4-8 seconds. **Breathe as slowly as you are comfortable with.** This is the rising arrow on the rectangle (see figure 1 below). Once your lungs reach their maximum compacity, pause for a moment, perhaps a second or two, briefly to your comfort. This is the top of the rectangle on the image provided. Feel the pressure. Listen without judgement.

Judgement means, if you hear a noise, you label it. You hear the dog barking and your mind says, "I have to feed sparky." To listen without judgement means to simply hear sounds as sound. To accomplish this when you hear something, focus back on your body and breath.

Gently release. As you are exhaling, again focus all your attention on the air leaving your nostrils or mouth. Feel and listen to your breath. This is the downward arrow on the image provided. Feel the pressure in your belly and chest release. While exhaling, imagine releasing all areas of tension in your body. Feel for your jaw, neck shoulders, fists, and feet. Imagine tension being released. If you don't feel the tension release, repeat these steps and lift your shoulders on the inhale. Allowing your shoulders to drop on every exhale will train your muscles to relax during this exercise.

While listening to the air and feeling the tension release, **you'll manage to press pause on the day**, even if only for a millisecond. This is beautiful. This is the present.

After a few rounds of Pause Breathing, during your exhale visualize that positive story you wrote. Dive into the story while performing more Pause Breaths. This is what the heart in the imagery stands for. You want to begin to plant real feelings of calm and positivity in your mind 10 or more times daily. If you are relaxed, you can focus all your attention on the positive thought.

The human lungs are long, deep lobes that create an area of "dead-space" where oxygen depleted air rests. To remove this dead air, when you are sitting comfortably, slowly exhale and force every bit of air out of your lungs. This may make you feel a little light-headed. Don't be alarmed. Clear your lungs out every so often and enjoy the rich deep breath that follows.

If you aren't getting a great oxygen rush upon inhale, or you're feeling short of breath despite having a clean set of lungs, really try to pull in as much air as possible on that inhale. You will be surprised how much you can fit in there and the increased oxygen will feel great on your body.

The last and most important tip to share is to not look over your shoulder and ask if anxiety is there. As we dive into how the mind is wired, you will understand that simply wondering if you are going to be anxious is the same thing as asking to be anxious. Focus 100% of your attention on the task at hand. It gets easier with time.

Practice makes perfect. Don't expect to get this right away. Remember, this is not a pill. This is a journey.

> *"I grew up around drugs, fighting, and sexual abuse. I want you to understand that no matter your story, life can be better. I started seeing change in just 2 weeks. After a month, no more panic attacks. Months after being coached by Khail and I can reflect on my past, not with heavy emotional attachment, but with gratitude and compassion. I see purpose. I am no longer driven by fear, depression or anxiety. I am not a victim."*
> **-Vanessa Perez**

The Pause Breath

Figure 1: The Pause Breath: From right to left, the up arrow signifies a long and deep belly breath inhale, the top is the pause, and the right side of the rectangle is a long and controlled exhale. Feel free to pause briefly before round 2 bottom of the rectangle. The heart signifies the story you wrote in this section.

Want a Video Tutorial? Check it out here! (Oldie but goodie)
https://youtu.be/VA9kH9qXn7s

Pause Breaths Expanded

"All of humanity's problems stem from man's inability to sit quietly in a room alone."
-Blaise Pascal

To really solidify this practice in the new lifestyle you are developing for yourself, let's go over some of the science and benefits of the Pause Breath.

First, you read correctly. This routine trained my muscles to beat sleep apnea. The muscle memory developed while performing this routinely will help develop deeper and more efficient breathing for you too. Pause Breaths get your entire body involved. It takes a lot of practice to develop this memory, but when you do, you barely have to put any conscious effort into it. It will be as easy as brushing your teeth. Now I yawn just by thinking about the Pause Breath. You will get there.

The posture: open shoulders, chin up, back erect, and palms open, tells the body there is no danger. Think of the soft spots on your body. These are your belly and your neck. By exposing these, you are telling your body that it is safe. There are no tigers around. The opposite is scientifically proven to cause symptoms of depression, elicit fear and can be detrimental to your health. Practicing the pause breaths will improve your mood and posture!

Deep belly breaths trigger the autonomic nervous system, which signals to the entire body and brain that everything is safe and forces you to begin to feel calm. **With practice, you will experience immediate relief and the ability to banish any panic attack before it gets too close.**

Pause breaths are fantastic at interrupting negative patterns, fear, phobias, and symptoms of anxiety. A "pattern interrupt" is necessary to break old habits. They are also perfect "starting rituals" which can be thought of as a positive trigger for every new positive experience you wish to have. This technique becomes like a pause and play button for the body to experience confidence and calm.

Apart from the chemical, neurological, strength and happy benefits the Pause Breaths will bring you, the increased oxygen and decreased heart rate will yield healthier blood-flow and blood-pressure! The regular bouts of calm will aid these as well.

Conscious belly breathing is our bridge to the subconscious mind. As mentioned before, it is something that can be both conscious and subconscious. This is the tool you will use to plant seeds into the mega-farm behind most of your decision making.

Above everything, being happy not only makes you feel better, it makes you smarter and helps you live longer (feel free to google the longest study in human history)! So, stay committed to this breathing exercise, minimum 10 times daily over the next 4 weeks and you will hardly recognize yourself!

Before going forward, what nerdy facts about this breathing technique are you going to focus on to help keep you consistent? List them below.

Why I'll Do Pause Breaths

_____

_____

_____

_____

_____

_____

> "Ever since I started working with Khail, my life has changed for the better, every single day. In the same way that anxiety used to take over, irrationally and forceful, I now experience the exact opposite. Surges of happiness that run through my body. Having suffered from repeated nightmares, I forgot what it was like to wake up rested. My triggers are a thing of the past. Thank you Khail. I love you, brother!
> **-Tanya Quintieri**

Anxiety Eliminating Routines

If it is holding you back from your happiness, it is an excuse.

To finish explaining the foundational work that will help you tackle anything that comes your way in this lifetime, I'll describe some of the key routines you need to develop for confidence and positivity.

The morning is a very special time. It is the moment you are coming out of unconsciousness. You have a clean slate. Your first thoughts and behaviors will start the trajectory for the rest of your day. The morning is usually very rough for those suffering from anxiety. Why? I'll have you answer this. Your answers will be very revealing. How do you start every morning? What are the first few things you do? What are some of your first **thoughts**?

_____

_____

_____

_____

_____

_____

_____

A very important tip! Anywhere you see life as difficult, it's wonderful, because these are the areas for most growth. In business, the 80/20 rule means you get 80% of your business from 20% of your best clients. This rule is universal. These select 20% areas of your life, those hard mornings specifically, carry your biggest upside for potential happiness in your life. Fixing them will change 80% of your problems!

So, every morning, **pop out of bed immediately** (have that notebook handy?). This is the hardest thing for people to commit to, but it is as simple as standing. Surely you can stand (although I've coached many that believed they couldn't stand).

If you put weight on it, tell yourself how tired you are or how poorly you feel, it will be way more difficult. When your alarm goes off, pretend you're a secret agent. Your bed will self-destruct in 3, 2, 1. Hop out of bed! Pretend you are a rocket ship and there's a countdown. Pretend you are the most motivated person you know, and you love springing out of bed. These ideas sound silly, but they work! They are scientifically proven to work. And this is how you will begin to change your behavior and rewire your mind for motivation and confidence.

The most important thing is to commit. Do not lounge around in bed for any reason. No matter the reason, it is an excuse. Hop out of bed and by the end of this journey, it will be much easier to do so.

When you get out of bed, you want to chug a big glass of water. This will get you started on drinking enough water for the day. It will also get your metabolism going and wake you up a little. I'm often surprised at how awake I feel when I don't drink coffee and instead drink a nice helping of water. Truth.

Do some stretching and light exercise. Do your Pause Breaths and think your positive thought. This will set your intention for the rest of the day!

The last thing to note about the morning is to refrain from going on social media, exposing yourself to any media or electronics for at least 20 minutes after waking up. Remember, you are setting your intention for the day and your intention is to be calm. Your email and social media are over-stimulating, they are pleasure seeking outside of yourself, and they are reminding you who you were, not promoting who you are becoming.

Below is an example of a morning routine checklist. Write this down for yourself or copy and print it to keep handy. A checklist is an excellent way of keeping you consistent!

Morning Checklist:

Hopped out of bed?
Pause Breaths: How long?
Water: How much?
Stretching & light exercise?
20mins no electronics?

Evening routines are equally important for disrupting negative patterns in your life. Nighttime is usually spent ruminating on all the bad in our lives. Note this. And keep your thoughts positive at night. Always go to bed on a good note. Make sure you stop exposing yourself to electronics at least 20 minutes before getting in bed. Why? Research blue light and remember what I said about stimulation. Do your Pause Breaths and allow yourself to focus on feeling well.

Evening Checklist:

No electronics for 20mins?
Pause Breaths: How many?
Today's Water: How much?
Stretching & light exercise?
Kept my thoughts clean?

Planting seeds of positivity is incredibly important for rewiring your mind for peace and calm. Know that if you are using sleep aids or self-medicating with booze, you are doing your mind a disservice. You are cheating the greatest system in the universe, your brain, by using something to calm you and help you sleep. Don't beat yourself up over this now. Baby-steps, but always take a little step.

Work towards being self-reliant and you will continue to grow.

Naturally getting to sleep and staying asleep can be difficult. In the next section, I will be discussing just how take care of this problem. For now, make sure you are keeping your checklists and taking this practice with you until your life is exactly where you want it to be! This foundation will ensure that the following, more difficult teachings stick. Without it, the house crumbles. So, stick with the foundation! I think you get it by now.

> *"I had been suffering with anxiety, Pure-O OCD and panic attacks for around 20 years. Thankfully, I met Khail. I wasn't sleeping or eating, hadn't been on the freeway in over 2 years and was avoiding crowded paces. Within 3 weeks I was sleeping again, my appetite was back, I got back on the freeway and had an amazing time at a mall! I'm better than I've ever been thanks to Khail. I cannot recommend him and his methods highly enough!"*
> **-Lisa Slater**

Curing Insomnia

"The less effort, the more powerful you will be."
-Bruce Lee

Insomnia can be a major hurdle when trying to beat anxiety but learning to sleep is a very basic skill. To go to sleep, one must let go. It isn't about trying to do something. Quite the opposite. If you want to gather sand, you must have a loose grip. If you squeeze, the sand will filter between your fingers and you will lose it. To grab hold of the sandman, don't NEED sleep. Don't put so much pressure on yourself.

For 29 years I suffered with PTSD related to sleep, insomnia, and then sleep apnea! I know this monster quite well, and what I can tell you is that the worst part about it was how seriously I took my sleep.

If you don't get enough sleep, is the world going to end? You will be tired, groggy and foggy. But this isn't something you're not used to. It isn't anything you haven't experienced a thousand times before, right? Be honest here. It sucks, but it isn't going to kill you to lose a night sleep here and there. We often take sleep too seriously. To be sincere, come to terms with this point first. Everything is going to be okay if you don't get the perfect night sleep.

Next, follow your evening routine by leaving the electronics off and away from you all night. If you wake up, don't check the time. **Don't count the hours or minutes you have left.** This will always lead to suffering. Simply roll over and go back to sleep. This is the part that hits home for so many people. If you wake up minutes before your alarm goes off, smile and say "good" because you have more time to practice your foundation, more pause breaths to take. This advice will change your life!

When you wake up and check your phone, the light from your phone stimulates your brain and makes your body believe it is daytime. The apps on your phone stimulate your mind and make it much more difficult to relax back to sleep. And simply the habit of waking up and looking at your phone is wiring your mind and body to do it again and again. It is an easy addiction to stop cold turkey. You can do this!

Remember, practice what you DO want, not what you don't.

When you are ready for sleep, get comfortable, and perform Pause Breaths, focusing only on the breathing. If you drift into thought, try counting your pause breaths. Calmly shift your focus back to breathing and never beat yourself up about slipping. Perform this technique each time you wake up in the middle of the night as well.

If you are lying in bed for more than 20 minutes, get up and do something inspiring, something you love, or journal. Plant a seed of positivity in your mind. More will be revealed later regarding the power of this healthy habit.

PRO TIP: Using the notebook you are definitely using right now, keep track of the thoughts and dreams that interest you. Journaling when you can't sleep to reflect on your mind and better understand how to change will prove enlightening.

Like anything, curing insomnia is a process. Be patient. Don't take it so seriously.

Want a tutorial on beating insomnia? Here's a clip from a mini-course I created!
https://youtu.be/hn4PPKOiAoQ

> *"I have come from a very dark place. At one point I was on 24hr watch by my friends and family. I couldn't leave the house, get out of bed, take my children to school, or perform my job, leaving my business partner hanging. I was completely medicated. Thousands of dollars later, psychologists and psychiatrists, ready to give up, I decided to work with Khail. It has changed my life and practically brings me to tears. Just saying his name makes me smile. I've completely turned my life around and Khail has been the only person to help me do that. You deserve it. Contact Khail."*
> **-Nicky Tong**

Developing Mindfulness

"Love is the only force capable of transforming an enemy into a friend."
-Martin Luther King Junior

The secret to beating anxiety is to combat it with the opposite. You fear anxiety, you hate panic you run from triggers, and their power only grows.

To beat anxiety, you need to train your body for calm. You need to experience calm, clarity, ease and love more often than you currently experience, and you need to do so by your own design.

As you master the pause breath, and I really mean master it, I mean that you need to commit to doing it so much that you develop calm as an easy reflex... As you master this technique, you will begin to develop more of a controlled mindfulness.

I say controlled because I look at anxiety as "absent-mindfulness". Anxiety fills our minds with nonsense, negativity and fear. It takes our attention away from everything we wish to experience and hones in on everything we do not. With control and focus, your entire perspective on life will change!

As you master the Pause Breath, you will be able to see your thoughts as they come to you, rather than notice them halfway through a terrible and irrational storyline playing out in your head, or the umpteenth hour you've stared at the dark ceiling.

Begin to take notice to the physical sensations in your body, not just when you are having an attack. Notice the tension you are carrying in your body. Allow the regular Pause Breaths to be a time for you to check in on your body, but in a way that says "can I feel better, calmer or happier?" Where are you tense? Is your stomach pulled in? How is your posture? In fact, any time you notice or think of breathing, do a deep belly breath and release tension!

Remember, an open and comfortable posture tells the mind and the body that everything is ok!

Notice how often you breathe shallow and how often you hold your breath. How is the quality of your breath right now?

Notice when you feel most anxious. Where are you physically regarding tension and posture, and where is your mind? What are your thoughts of? Every time you notice that you feel off, celebrate! I mean it. I want you to see these things as a good thing. Why? Khail why on earth would I want to see any of this as a good thing? I feel terrible about it.

While walking the path towards betterment, notice where you trip.

See, the subconscious mind is like a garden. You've planted crops every time you have good experiences, positive thoughts, and confident feelings.

But you've also planted *craps* every time you experience something negative. Now, these weeds are all over the place and it is up to you to see them and replace them with something loving, positive, inspiring and happy. You don't want a bunch of craps in your garden.

Every time you have a poor experience, you can rest assured that you haven't arrived at inner-peace just yet, that you still have room for growth, and unless you feel like a 10 out of 10 all day every day, you're going to want to notice these areas of lack in your life and replace them. Right? If you don't feel like life is perfect, isn't it a great thing to see room for improvement?

Your every action is cultivation for life's garden.

Your triggers are weeds. Triggers are ridiculous. We are living in a society where we slap five over our ailments and keep our strengths under wraps. We are embarrassed to feel great about something we are amazing at, fearing that others will judge us negatively. Yet we are so quick to beat ourselves up over anything wrong with us, and usually so quick to share our shortcomings. This goes back to our primal survival instincts and how the mind is wired, and it robs your joy.

Attack your triggers with as much positivity and love as you can muster! Each trigger is a perfect time to practice your new techniques! I say they're ridiculous because you are far too powerful to have triggers! Trust me. You will have more practical applications for trigger-crushing as you work through this program, but for now, try to reframe, see a different perspective or seek the silver-lining.

Inside of us there lives two wolves. We feed these wolves our thoughts. The bad wolf feeds on everything negative. Every feeling of jealousy. Every time we are afraid or anxious, this wolf is fed. When we are angry, feel **guilty**, or embarrassed, this is bad wolf food. And when we beat ourselves up and pity ourselves, we are feeding the bad wolf.

Then there's the good wolf. The wolf that feeds on laughter, joy and presence. This wolf grows stronger with every goal you accomplish, every time you surprise yourself and every experience you relish in.

The good wolf and the bad wolf go to war every night. Which wolf will win? How will your reality, your state-of-being, be defined? By feeding one of the wolves more than the other. Starve that bad wolf by feeding the good wolf!

Frequently ask yourself: which wolf am I feeding?

Bonus #1: Over-the-Top Silliness Challenge

I am adding a few bonus materials to this book to help motivate and energize you! Adopting at least one of these bonus practices daily will help wire for the positive experience you wish to make your way of life. This technique only takes a few seconds to a minute to perform!

Start by getting somewhere private, or if you don't mind being socially awkward, choose a place where you can make a scene! Loosen up and then jump up and down a few times. Pretend your favorite sports team just won, you won the lottery, or you're an absolute nutjob jumping for joy because the aliens are coming. Whatever visual you need to get started, focus on that.

While jumping and celebrating, immerse yourself in the experience. Shout "yay" and "yes" and do some arm gestures that go along with this behavior. The key is to act your way into excitement. The result: you will feel really, really good from doing about 20 seconds of a pretend cheer. If you truly try your hardest, you will feel good.

Ask yourself how often you actually have this much fun. By doing this every day for just a moment or for a few moments multiple times a day, you will tip the scales of your experience and overall state-of-being to be more positive, you will prove to yourself that your state is within your grasp, you will elicit the chemicals you're looking for, and you may even manage to make others feel uncomfortable!

This may sound silly, but it is the first bonus because it truly is very effective. Do this with your pets or your children. Force your spouse or your friends to do it. Have fun. Life is short. Don't take it too seriously. And add this to your daily regimen for creating the version of you that you're growing towards.

"Khail has a true gift. He's able to shift through to not put band-aids on bullet holes but to find the source of the shooting. He's helped me break through multiple glass ceilings. Whether you want relief from yourself or just want more from life, Khail is incredible."
-Dr. Chris Lee

Brag Book

The space below will continue to inspire you along your journey and will be very powerful to reflect on in a few weeks when you see just how much you have accomplished. **Use the first lines to describe your current state, challenges, opinions and perspectives of your situation as it is today.** Where and when do you struggle? How do you sleep? What are your mornings like? How are your relationships? In a few weeks, you won't even recognize your old self. Once you've finished that, use the spaces in your brag book to write down every accomplishment, no matter how small! Examples could include, "I got out of bed right when my alarm went off without hitting snooze!", "I smiled more today than I have in years", or "I drove, and it was amazing!" YOU WANT TO USE THIS! It will be SO VERY HELPFUL!! Don't make me quote Arnold again.

Do You Want to Be Right or Happy?

When climbing the ladder of life, the best way to let go of what's beneath you is to reach for the rung above you.

When working in the trenches, in the depths of thousands of suffering souls, in the bowels of Facebook groups devoted to perpetuating the negativity, I use this question as an eye-opening lesson. Someone that has read every book on mental health, someone that knows the gut-flora and every chemical pathway published, someone that has been through hell and continues to live it, will usually have a hard time believing that they can get better. That difficulty they experience often translates to animosity.

And for good reason. Look at how hard they are trying to find a cure. They are putting every effort, every ounce of energy, every resource, into finding a cure. The trouble is, they are looking in one direction. Like a horse wearing blinders, they will run straight down one path until the path runs right up to a cliff. Then they will stop. Firmly. They believe that if they take another step, they'll go nowhere. Afterall, there's nothing in front of them. This is called "learned helplessness", and is a term used to describe this stuck feeling. Some amazing research has been done on this phenomenon, but the only thing that is important to note for you right now is what can be learned, can be unlearned.

Shift your perspective slightly and an entirely new path will be revealed.

Perhaps this sounds like you? Good. It means we have more in common than you may think.

When I was experiencing regular panic attacks, my depression was worse than ever. I wasn't sleeping. I wasn't eating enough. I wasn't well. I was miserable. And it felt like the world was against me.

The thoughts of suicide were TOO normal. They were casual contemplations like deciding which pair of shoes to wear or what movie to watch. I was talking about it with my wife as if to brace her for the inevitable like it was a conversation about taxes. I'd carry these thoughts with me everywhere and act like I was fine. I never thought that *I* could do anything different.

In a hard cry, with my face on the floor, I realized I just wanted to be happy. I had always been right about everything. My childhood, work and personal relationships, anytime there was a fight, I was right. But I was never happy. I wanted to lobotomize myself. I wanted to smash my head into a wall and forget how to be clever. I wanted to dumb myself down as much as I needed to live the rest of my life happily.

I knew that none of this seemed practical, but something snapped in my mind. I realized that there are different perspectives. We as humans are a collection of perspectives. If you think about doctors, we have specialists because the human body is so complex. But the mind is the most complex system in the entire universe. And it isn't just a mind. It is everything. Everything we do, every science, every math, every song, and every perspective we gather from other people, they all come from this same mind structure and they are all being filtered through the mind. It is biased, and often blinded by emotion. Amazing really to understand our entire reality is fabricated through this fear-seeking lens.

I noticed that there's a ton of confliction in science and psychology from reactionary and proactive approaches. There's psychiatry and psychology. There's neurology and neuroscience and all the specifics in these fields. Then, it isn't just a brain disease we are talking about here is it? It's the full body. It's the gut. Its personality and consciousness. Scientifically speaking, we have no definitive answer to the question "what is consciousness?"

I realized that I was only thinking in a reactionary mindset. Treating a problem.

I didn't want to treat a problem. I wanted to create a solution.

Once I acquired the mindset for seeking solutions, the answers revealed themselves. I realized that I had to be wrong about most things. I had to let go of the "truths" I was so desperately clinging to. Stuff like "it's my anxiety that stops me from doing xyz."

So, whenever you feel tension, ask "do I want to be right or do I want to be happy?"

Sure, the doctor said you have major depression, but how does that make you feel? How are these feelings **SERVING** you? Asking yourself "how does this serve me" is possibly the most powerful questions you can ask. Write it down. Take it with you everywhere you go. Ask it in situations, during thoughts and feelings, before any sort of investments, and before you decide to get into a debate with someone.

Sure, your spouse is off base or being mean, but how does it make you feel when you retaliate. When you fight and fight, do you go to sleep happy? How does it feel to try to make them into the person you want them to be?

Sure, traffic has delayed your trip, your car isn't your first choice, your kids aren't adorable enough, your dog smells (having fun here). Sure, you're justified to feel the way you feel or say the things you NEED to say, but do they make you happy?

If being right, if feeling validated or justified is more important than your happiness, you will forever wire your mind for more negativity. You can't get to where I am and where the people I have helped are if this validation is more important to you than being happy. Take a moment to digest this.

So, choose happiness, calm, peace, love over everything and your entire experience, your life, what you view as reality, will slowly shape into something beautiful. If you're genuinely content, the rest of the world around you will benefit. Make a conscious decision, a firm affirmation, a hard commitment right now to choose happiness!

In the spaces below, write down some repeat offenses, typical arguments or discussions in your life that you are justified to have, but don't necessarily make you happy. When you're finished, write your commitment to happiness below them. If you are up for an early challenge, begin to reframe them to better serve you! Rewrite these to shine a positive light, a beacon of hope or some clarity to see the silver lining and just how this is all part of your amazing journey.

_____

_____

_____

_____

_____

_____

_____

_____

_____

_____

_____

_____

_____

_____

_____

_____

_____

_____

_____

_____

_____

_____

_____

_____

_____

_____

_____

_____

_____

_____

_____

> *"I have had panic attacks for 20+ years. I couldn't drive, leave my house, and had no control of my life. I was tapering off a heavy dose of benzos, couldn't sleep, and life was spiraling. That is when I met Khail. His advice is amazing. I'm driving, sleeping, mending relationships with family members I thought were forever broken, and best of all, he helped me taper so fast and with minimal anxiety. I now have the tools to beat panic and remain benzo-free. All because of Khail's coaching!"*
> **-Jody Waite**

Attention Defines Reality

"When you change the way you look at things,
the things you look at change."
-Dr. Wayne Dyer

In life, our experience is a choice. It is truly up to us to decide whether something is good or bad. With time, you will know it in your heart. Calculus or aeronautical schematics (fun word) may look like gibberish to you, but that doesn't mean that there isn't truth in those notes. How *you* see things doesn't define reality.

So, let me help you to open your eyes. Everyone is familiar with Where's Waldo. The artist has cleverly hidden this little man with a striped hat in a sea of similar looking objects and people. As you scan your eyes across the image, you are **intending** to find the only Waldo that exists.

Everything that looks just like Waldo pops out at you. Your attention is drawn to the Waldo-like images. If after finding Waldo I covered the image, you would have very little recollection of the rest of the scene because you only had one intention: to find Waldo.

Our attention in life defines the intention behind our experience.

We create an intention, as if to intend to find the things that we give the most attention to. If you think about how this program was created, it is a really good thing for us to be extra perceptive of any tiger looking objects. The fear for a tiger creates the tiger-seeking experience. We miss the bigger picture very easily because of this. And for good reason. It's very efficient. The mind is efficient at finding what we are seeking, and thus ignoring what we are not.

In fact, the mind is too efficient. You will **always** find what you are looking for. But this is on an emotional level, not thoughts. Remember that the mind and body speak in feelings.

What are you paying attention to right now? What thoughts are cycling through your head regularly? How are you typically feeling about situations or triggers? Remember to be interrupting the harmful patterns with your Pause Breaths and positive thought insertion. Remember that the negative is your upside potential.

Researchers split up two groups of people based on their beliefs. One group believed they were lucky. A lot of us know these types of people. They get out of tickets, find money randomly, or always seem to be getting promotions or compliments.

The other group believed that they were unlucky. This was the old Khail. I truly believed I was cursed. My father called it the Kapp curse. "No matter what we do in life, we will always get the brunt end", he'd say. And it was true for the longest time.

Until, of course, I changed my beliefs.

The unlucky group has beliefs that things won't work out, they can't catch a break and the world is against them.

The researchers walked the groups through an area on the way to the supposed testing facility. Secretly, this walk was the study, and they had placed money all over to see who would notice it. The lucky group found the money and the unlucky group didn't notice it at all.

How can this be? Surely the unlucky group wants money more than the other, right? But the understanding here is that the unlucky group *believes* they would never be so lucky as to find a $50 bill on the ground.

When they want for money, they *feel* terrible. That feeling translates into thoughts of lack. The feelings outweigh their conscious desires and create a belief system that blinds them from noticing anything that would go against it. Are you following? Your thoughts and inner-dialog will be dwarfed by your emotions. Your limbic system reigns supreme until you get ahead of it with mindfulness.

There are tons of studies where people get healthier, lower cholesterol and blood pressure, heal faster and even heal things that are technically **medically impossible** all due to a positive change in belief systems.

Through our senses, the brain absorbs about 400B bits of information every single second. But our conscious minds, how we define ourselves, who we are at any given moment, is only a mere... are you ready for this... 2,000 bits of information every second. This number can hardly even be looked at as significant, yet here we are, living through a peep-hole of reality. Basically, we aren't remotely aware of 1% of the environment and experience that our brain is absorbing, that our subconscious mind is taking in at any given moment. We aren't significantly aware of what the subconscious chooses to show us. What could you be missing in your reality right now?

Why do you hear your name across a loud party? Why do you see a child walking on the sidewalk while you're driving? How do we find Waldo?

Our intention in life defines our reality.

To create an intention that you want to experience, to see the silver lining, to experience hope, to light the path towards your healing, **pay attention to what you actually want to experience.** You hear your name across the party because you've given that title plenty of attention; you have an intention to hear your name. You will create the life you wish to experience by beginning to apply these principals to every moment of your life. By not playing a victim of circumstance, you are choosing your destiny. I will dig into this more as the lessons get deeper.

You can live the life you want by diverting your attention towards positivity over and over.

Right now, you are suffering. Taking anxiety as an example, as you notice it or think about it, it gets worse. It goes something like "I really hope I don't have a panic attack tonight in front of my friends. That would be terrible and embarrassing. Oh, great now my heart is starting to race! Now it's faster? You've got to be kidding me! Why is this happening to me now? I'm feeling dizzy, I hope I don't pass out." Boom panic attack ensues.

While performing the Pause Breath, it is important to use this understanding of attention and anxiety. If you are wondering why you are feeling anxious, you are feeding your mind anxiety. If you are wondering whether you will have anxiety later, you're going to start to feel it now. And if you start to talk about the absence of anxiety, you will be giving it presence. You are literally inviting anxiety in! If you're struggling with the breathing, what kind of attention are you giving it?

I know I ask a ton of questions, but I want to urge you to step back and think about them. You have your answers inside of you. Allow me to spark your awareness of your mind and body.

The more you understand yourself, the faster you will master.

So, you need to start redefining reality for your best intentions. The best version of you! Start telling yourself that you live in a friendly world. That there is SO MUCH good out there. Start looking for it, and in time, your mind will help you see it.

What good can you see hidden in your fears? Example: Health Anxiety. How does your family's medical history HELP you feel healthier? When have you proven to yourself that you are healthy and able bodied? Have doctors told you that you were healthy? What can you notice from day-to-day that PROVES you are healthy? Below, write down your fear(s) and list reasons why it is better to think positive. List facts that can help you feel good, and anything else that can tip the scales towards a better belief system.

_____

_____

_____

_____

_____

_____

_____

_____

_____

_____

_____

Bonus #2: So Be It

Congrats! You've unlocked your second bonus! Your homework for this section is to put the phone down. **Go outside for a few minutes every day** and just be without cigarettes, a drink, or anything in your hands. Don't bring the kids or the dog. Just breathe and look around slowly. Notice the stillness, the peace, and the overall contentment of the world around you. Find it!

Note: If you can't get outside yet and that is your goal with this program, I want you to get to a window or stand on the porch and get a taste of *real* reality every day. Disconnect from all the chatter. Just simply be.

Defining the "Right" Attention

"The most important decision we make is deciding whether we live in a friendly or hostile universe."
-Albert Einstein

The more you think something, the more you pay attention to the same things and the more you experience these things the same way, the way you've experienced your entire life, the easier it gets to experience them. Think of a specific fear you have. If you go through the same thoughts and feelings process with it again and again, it just becomes harder wired in your beliefs. Practice feeling something enough and you will begin to believe it. Makes sense, right?

Let's step back for a moment. What do you think feelings are? What do you think you are *feeling*? How can you *feel* happiness? Why do you *feel* sadness? Your feelings are chemicals. If your thoughts can create feelings, then your thoughts can trigger chemical releases in your body. Do you feel something when watching a scary movie, even though it is just a trillion lights and sound waves? You know it is just an electronic device emitting sensory signals, but you *allow* yourself to become immersed in it. You'll jump. You'll feel! You may even have nightmares. I remember a scary movie I watched when I was a child. I carried the fear from that movie for weeks! Surely, you are capable of changing the levels and the balances of these chemicals just by changing your thoughts if a screen can affect you this dramatically.

If you suffer from chemical imbalances, why wouldn't balancing those chemicals be like going to the gym or practicing an instrument or researching a new subject? If thoughts create feelings, why wouldn't practiced thoughts lead to practiced feelings?

The key word here is **PRACTICE.** With practice, it gets easier to feel fear or to feel confidence. Without practice, you're just trying to pull a fast one over the old subconscious mind (which will never work). Just thinking positive is empty without feeling.

Here's a great example of how thoughts turn into chemicals. I want you to sit back and imagine that I just prepared for you a fresh pizza. If you don't like pizza, this might still work, but pick a different food. So, I'm pulling this pizza out of the brick oven and instantly you are hit with these overwhelming smells. This rich aroma of cheese and garlic tickles your nostrils. The sound of the sizzling cheese and steam rising from the crust radiates in your ears. The crust is crispy, but not overdone. The cheese is stretchy but held together. I hand you the perfect slice. You bite into it and realize this is the best pizza you've ever had.

Is your mouth watering? Do you FEEL like you are ready for that pizza? Well your body, your subconscious mind, nearly 95% of you believes there is pizza right here and right now. In your saliva, you're releasing a carbohydrate digesting enzyme called amylase. Enzymes and hormones are released from your body based on the body's beliefs. If the majority of what you call "me" truly believes there's pizza here from a short description, a commercial, or a memory, what else do you think you are capable of believing? What doesn't exist in the present that you can still feel or experience easily? Plenty of bad memories perhaps? What amazing thing in life do you think you could experience with the right attention? Take a moment to allow these questions to brew in that big beautiful brain of yours and write down some thoughts below. It is VERY important to slow down and prove to yourself that you are growing, and you are capable.

What Positive Belief *Could* I Experience with the Right Attention?

_____

_____

_____

_____

_____

Pizza is practiced for most of us. We can't be in the middle of the most stressful situation of our lives and expect to do this by thinking about an imaginary meadow or a calming waterfall. I wouldn't expect you to be able to go from a driving phobia to imagining you are a professional stunt driver. You can! Don't get me wrong. But I want to show you the smoothest path.

With practice, you can allow yourself to believe anything. To experience anything! And what are beliefs? They are what defines you. Your beliefs are you, cut to the core. So, your attention to things, not just your level of attention, but the way you see them, the WAY you experience, will ultimately define who you are.

> *"All that we that are is a result of what we have thought."*
> -Buddha

> *"Be careful how you think, for your life is shaped by your thoughts."*
> Proverbs 4:23

Playing the same songs in your head, rehearsing your fears over and over will consume you. Rehearsing is a good word here, because IT IS a practice. And we need to change your practice. You need to practice more of the experiences that feel good and serve you. You need to practice enjoying your life in ALL areas. **You need to practice calm.**

Why practice? Why does practice make perfect? Why does Khail keep using the word practice?!

The wiring of the connections in your mind, the neural networks, work very much like power lines or the wiring in your house. The rubber on the outside of the wire, the insulation makes the movement of electricity efficient. The thicker the rubber, the more efficient the current, and thus the smoother (easier/faster) the pathway.

Right now, in your life, you have practiced behaviors that come to you so naturally, they require little to no thought. They've become instinctual. The more you practice, the thicker the myelin sheath, or the thicker the insulation becomes around neural pathways. This isn't just in the mind, but the body as well, throughout your entire nervous system. Ever notice how quickly you react if someone throws something towards you? Or if something falls in front of you, notice how quickly you reach out to catch it? What about how easily your body might go into a panic attack?

Think about driving, or better yet, brushing your teeth. How often are you consciously aware that you are brushing each individual tooth versus how often are you just allowing the routine to take place, allowing the program to operate on auto-pilot, while you worry or think about something "productive"?

The mind optimizes, remember? We do something until it has become such a practiced effort that we literally "program" our mind and body to perform it without "our" intervention.

You must simply write a better program.

Anxiety, worry, fear, blame, guilt, stress, anger, whatever it is, has become a practiced routine in your body. Often, people experience panic attacks without being triggered or thinking about anything. The body panics as a practiced reflex.

Think of your mind like roadways. The practiced behaviors are speedy highways. When you're learning to let go of the bad and focus on the good, you are going from a nice, smooth highway, to an old country road.

There are going to be bumps, potholes, and the occasional cow blocking your path. But, as you travel this road again and again, your ride becomes easier and smoother. You will turn these new thoughts, these calming and loving behaviors into a speedy highway! **Just keep driving on the road you wish to travel.**

Pain versus Suffering

"Your familiar memories related to your known world "re-mind" you to reproduce the same experiences."
-Dr. Joe Dispenza

I'm hiking with a friend in the mountains above northern Hollywood, California, when I nearly step on a baby rattlesnake. I wear toe shoes. Your foot has 28 joints and even more ligaments that aren't being used correctly in a shoe. Don't judge me. Anyway, I put one of these socially awkward shoes right above this baby snake and almost came down all the way. It reared up and bit my foot. As I lay there dying, I realize that the bite hurt a lot, but the poison is what was causing me long term suffering. Moments before I died, I realized that telling a fake story to prove a point might not work. Okay so the snake didn't bite me. Luckily! But the rest did happen. I didn't notice it until the last second! And the younger the snake, the more toxic the venom, because they're not accurate yet. It didn't even rattle. I snapped a few pics and talked to it for a moment before it slithered away.

There's an important difference between pain and suffering. Nobody ever died from a snakebite. It is the venom that is the slow killer. The snakebite is the poor experience, something someone did that hurt you or something you thought that threw you off. The venom, this poison that travels through your entire being, this is fueled by your attention to the painful experience, your ruminating and reminiscing, your worrying and hating. The truth is, right here in this present moment, you are not being bit. But if you are suffering, it is because you are reliving the experience again and again. You relive it with your thoughts and feelings. Reliving is literal. Your entire being believes this experience is happening. The same chemicals are released. The same hard-wired thought patterns are used. Your very core KNOWS that the trauma is happening again, even though it isn't.

This practiced effort can be repeated all throughout your life. But it doesn't have to be.

Pain might be mandatory, but suffering is optional.

I like to look at it like a wound. A wound, with the right treatment, will always heal all by itself. The body will take care of that wound. But it is our constant attention to that wound, the picking at the scab or the removal of the bandages again and again that will cause infection. When you check on the wound to see if it is healed, you're exposing it again. Do you follow?

What is it in your life that you are giving negative attention to? Is there something inevitable? Something like a job, a family member, that time of the month, or some chronic pain that you are consistently revisiting with the WRONG kind of attention? Think about this for a moment and jot down some of these repeat offenders.

My Repeat Offenders List

_____

_____

_____

_____

_____

_____

_____

_____

These consistent experiences you are giving the wrong attention to are hard-wiring who you are, to be much more of "that". If you live in misery for one week out of every single month, or half of every day, you may begin to understand why it has been so difficult to break the cycle of fear in your life! Ah hah moment?

Remember, pain might be mandatory, but the suffering is optional. As you practice the Pause Breaths and positive thought insertion, you are probably noticing that you are becoming more mindful and able to separate yourself from your thoughts and feelings, even if only slightly. **After 2 weeks of this practice, you will see your skills sharpening.** At any moment when you catch yourself, you can change the subject. You can decide to change that same old song playing in your head. You can choose to get off the subconscious loopdeloop.

Your homework here is to think about the "same old songs" that have been playing in your head. Your fears and worries, your hate, your pain and phobias. Write down any pity or guilt you typically feel. How are you talking to yourself? Putting this on paper should help to show you how ridiculous and harmful it is to rehearse these things.

Once you've defined some of these same old songs, you are going to want to start rewriting the music, and you will learn how over the next few sections! You will continue to see more songs over the next few weeks as your awareness expands, so come back to this and lay it all out.

Same Old Songs List

_____

_____

_____

_____

_____

_____

_____

_____

_____

_____

_____

_____

_____

_____

_____

_____

_____

"Since I've had the pleasure of meeting and working with Khail, he has totally changed my life!!! I knew from the second we spoke that he was going to be the person who would be able to help me. I've tried everything and anything to try and help myself through many years! My life used to be negativity, panic attacks, fear and constant worry, to now looking at life through beautiful eyes that see the positivity of life around me every day. I finally feel free from all the negativity that was holding me back for more than 30 years, and it is all because of Khail! This could change your life forever!"
-Laura Ann

Responsibility

You are what you eat.

When you squeeze an orange what comes out? What about if I squeeze that orange? What about if a car runs it over? What if you throw the orange against the wall, what comes out then? It's always orange juice, right?

No matter what happens on the outside, whatever it is that is already on the inside, is what comes out. It doesn't matter if your mom guilt-trips you, or you see a frightening story on the news, or your boss fires you, what comes out of you was already inside of you.

This is a huge lesson and a hard pill for many to swallow. But, if you've been keeping up with the breathing and mindfulness techniques for a week or so, you may be able to notice your *responsibility* here.

You see, we are responsible for what comes out of us because we are the security checkpoint for what goes into us. We are the gatekeepers of our experience.

Everything in your life is a result of how you choose to experience. Yes, you were innocent as a child and frankly you were innocent before you picked up this book too, but your innocence doesn't relieve you of your suffering, does it?

Forget the justification. Rather than validate WHY you feel bad, look at HOW you can experience today better. Look at the foundation and rituals you've begun and see that you are doing WHAT it takes to get out of this. If the validation doesn't serve you, if it doesn't make you feel good, why continue to validate?

You are no longer a victim of circumstance.

We are all responsible for everything that happens in our lives. But responsibility isn't about blame or fault. It isn't about right or wrong either. Responsibility is just our "response-ability"; our ability to respond.

If you and I took a vacation together. We could have entirely different experiences. We could do the exact same things, eat the same foods, have the same schedule etc., but we could experience the vacation completely differently based very much on the quality of our attention to the experience.

If someone is yelling, and it has nothing to do with you, you have the ability to respond. You can ask them to be quiet, you can think to yourself "that guy is horrible" and you can carry that experience around with you. You could even pull out some popcorn and watch, or you could decide to turn your attention to something you enjoy. These are all responses, and although they may not seem like this right now, they are all within your ability.

Why do some cancer patients seem like the happiest people in the world? How do people go on living successful and happy lives after child abuse? How do some soldiers come home from war without any stress disorder? Why do kids let things go so quickly?

Well, children haven't learned to validate their misery yet. That is one bad lesson we adults teach them. Before they learn this, they just want to have fun and be happy. They've got it all figured out. As for the rest, and the kids, if they can do it, so can you.

In time you will understand that your experience is in your hands. You will know it in your core. The more mindful you become, the more awake to this reality you'll become and the more choice you will have. Your conscious effort becomes your reality. In the next section, I am going to break down exactly how to make the right choice!

> *"I have the tools to relieve myself of anxiety and panic after 17 years of anxiety, panic and depression. At times, I wasn't able to eat or swallow, leave the house, or get out of bed. But within weeks I was changing and now my life is completely different! I am involved with all my daughter's softball games and we travel nationwide! I am sleeping, healthier and happier, and best of all, I have control! I used to have 8-12 panic attacks a day that weren't even triggered, and now I can guide myself away from anxiety before the symptoms even get bad. My family and I are so grateful for Khail! I strongly recommend anyone to give Khail a moment of your time."*
> **-April Gonzalez**

Experience is Choice: Right versus Higher Truth

If you seek it, you will find it, even if it isn't really there.

In life, there's always more than one way to look at things. For our purposes we will separate them into two categories called "right" and "higher truth".

What's right is what can be proven. What can be validated and justified. It's what the doctors tell you. It is how you were raised and what your parents have led you to believe. Sometimes, what is right is simply that, it *is* right. But what is "right" may not be the entire truth, and it may not serve any purpose apart from validation.

Sometimes, being right sucks. If you are arguing with your spouse and you're completely right, do you automatically feel good? Does arguing, fighting, or complaining automatically bring you more peace or love? You may think that filling that "need" to explain will yield a desired result but think about how most of your arguments end. In joyous laughter?

Remember how the mind works. The brain is an absorption machine and it is constantly optimizing. The brain continuously tries to turn bumpy country roads into speedy highways. It wants to make sure that the next time you experience anger, frustration, or panic, it is easier and faster to experience.

Being right doesn't always feel good, and practicing this "need" to justify will only program your mind to justify and feel poorly, again and again.

Ever wonder how some people just let problems roll off their shoulders? It is the same problem, yet to them, it doesn't carry as much weight. You may catch yourself trying to encourage them to feel worse about the problem because you can't comprehend how lightly they are taking it. In a way, either by choice or simply by their original programming, they are seeing things from a different perspective. Their perspective doesn't carry the emotional weight that yours might.

Now, allow me to me introduce to you THE perspective you are ready for! The higher truth. The "higher truth" is what serves your higher self, the version that you are growing towards. It may not feel good during the heat of the moment, or the first few times you try to walk that path, but it IS the way you want to experience because it serves you and makes you feel better or brings you wisdom. The higher truth is the piece you want to search for when you are in a situation that is bringing you discomfort.

Ask yourself, where is the higher truth here?

Imagine you're driving, and someone is tailgating you. They're way too close for your comfort, they're beeping and hollering at you. You could illegally brake-check them. Why not? You're justified. But what happens next? They get angrier. Or worse, you cause an accident. Ok, you don't brake-check, but perhaps you get really annoyed.

You wind up carrying that anger with you all day, making sure you share this story with your coworkers, friends and family, the same way caveman Bob told everyone about the tiger.

You could let the actions or words of someone else disrupt your entire day or worse. Or, you could seek the **higher truth**. You could seek your happiness above everything. You could flip up your mirror, ignore captain hurry and listen to a good song. You could pull over, send them your love, and allow them to be on their way. Then calm your emotions by feeding your mind this higher truth, knowing that this path is so much easier, flowing, and better for your growth.

Can you see how this changes everything? The same process can be done as thoughts pop into your head. **Start asking yourself, how does being right make me feel? How do I want to feel? Where's the higher truth here?**

It isn't just the outside world where we can seek higher truths. In fact, it is much more important to focus and improve that inner-dialog!

We have all heard "where there is a will, there is a way", but are we applying this to our lives? Can you see how this is true in the negative direction? Where there is a place to get angry, or offended, where there is a place to feel empty or tossed aside, do you ensure that you feel that way? Is there a particular person you MUST get angry at? Is there something you MUST avoid? For most of my life I craved this confrontation. I was addicted to being annoyed. Remember, you are not a victim of circumstance and you want your happiness above everything. **List a few times being right didn't feel good. Then describe the higher truth.** Tell yourself that you will choose this road next time and visualize it. Keep aiming for that higher truth.

Right Reframed to Higher Truth

_____

_____

_____

_____

_____

_____

_____

The term "cognitive dissonance" is the experience felt when one is trying to improve, but they feel like they are fighting themselves. Be it procrastination, blame, guilt or fear, sometimes we will start to seek problems with our teachers or mentors, some will say it was because "I was raised this way", "how do you expect me to act like a saint when so-and-so is doing that", or "that's why I just *can't* move forward."

Maybe you're too tired to get out of bed or you've had a rough day so getting drunk tonight seems more useful than doing something quiet and healthy. Maybe work is rough, and you can't do your breathing? The higher truth here is that you can do anything you WANT to do. Your behavior is always your choice. And the moment you take responsibility for it, no matter how painful it may seem initially, will be the moment you turn everything around. I know it is hard. Break your patterns with your Pause Breaths! What better place than here? What better time than now?

The course of life's journey is plotted by our choices in every moment.

The warning here is that the smarter or cleverer you are, the more of a maze your subconscious mind is. You have barriers that you're not able to see. Programs in place to keep you from seeing and seeking the higher truth. You must not make excuses. **Excuses need to be defined as anything that keeps you from the higher truth.** I know. They are reasons. But, they are also validations to keep you where you are. All I want is to guide you to where you want to grow. Your subconscious will stop at nothing to protect your current identity. You must be mindful of this internal resistance.

One of the most common phenomena I've seen is a desperate fight to hang onto anxiety, old habits and other self-harming programs. Nearly every client I've worked with has broken down in a very confused cry only to realize they are sad to see their pain and suffering go away.

It sounds wild, but it is something you are going to want to be prepared for. **You want to remind yourself every single day why you are on this path.** Remind yourself what lies on the other side of this mountain. **Below, write with FEELING on what life will be like for you when you master your well-being!** Think about how this will affect others, your health, your passion or views on life. Take time to visualize as this is incredibly important.

My Beautiful Life Without Anxiety Looks Like:

_____

_____

_____

_____

_____

_____

_____

_____

_____

_____

_____

_____

_____

> *"After the first 2 weeks I was seeing some incredible changes in myself! I stopped worrying altogether! I began to relax!! This was a big deal for me because I've always carried so much tension in my body. By week 3 my fibromyalgia was gone! I was jumping out of bed and couldn't believe this could help me so much. The best thing is my life long anxiety and depression has just faded away. If it ever starts to bother me, I know just how to overcome it! I'm stronger, healthier, more peaceful and grateful than ever before! This has truly changed my life and I know it will for you too."*
> **-Rebekah Pierce**

Experience is Relative

"Although the world is full of suffering, it is also full of overcoming it."
-Helen Keller

I have heard the most unthinkable stories of the suffering people have endured. Experiencing the pain people carry has opened my eyes to a very important lesson. **Never compare.** Never compare yourself, your situation, your relationship, or anything else. Don't compare with your spouses, tallying up who does what. This is a mindset of evening out suffering, as if partners need to suffer equally. Where our heads go sometimes... Don't compare with your friends. This is wishing less on them or creating distance between you both. Comparing will always lead to suffering. See, we all experience life our own way. We can have entirely different experiences yet share the same familial blood, have the same upbringing and even be in the exact same environment. It doesn't matter.

Some people are happy despite cancer and some people are miserable despite financial and health abundance. It never matters. And when we compare our problems to others, even if we see that their problems are somehow worse, it doesn't change the way we feel. Growing up poor, we never had much to eat. And my mother would tell me to be grateful because there were starving children in Africa. Are you familiar with this one? It never made me excited to know there was more suffering. It will not make you feel better seeing suffering and it obviously won't make you feel better seeing other's happiness and comparing it to your situation.

The truth is, everyone can only see the world through their own lenses. We all have our own unique perspectives shaped by so many variables. One person's ease is definitely another person's suffering. What you may deem as your most challenging situations, others feel that same emotional weight for something completely different. I've seen a woman panic from PTSD resulting from falling down a cliff and awakening from a 3-month coma, and I've seen a man in panic because his girlfriend purchased the wrong coffee for him one too many times. It is all relative.

So, it is best to give people the benefit of the doubt, to not assume, to not compare, and focus on ourselves. It is all the same suffering. It all sucks. Remember that seeking empathy is feeding the bad wolf and will only perpetuate the problem. I used to want people to feel bad for me, to know my trauma and pain, until I realized that it meant that I wanted people to feel bad.

Let's push forward and create the solution, rather than spend another moment in this problem.

Avoid comparing from now on, and you will be avoiding a tremendous unnecessary burden. It takes practice. It's a process. Let's push forward!

> *"Khail has a way of speaking and wording things that really hit home. I have literally memorized several things he has said to me that when I'm having a negative day, can help me to turn things around in my mind to have a better outlook. His attention to your personal situation makes you feel like you have a close friend to confide in. He truly cares, unlike a general textbook answer to everything, he gives personalized advice and tailors it to whatever "issue" you're dealing with. Thank you, Khail, for helping me focus more on the present and learning to just "dance with" and accept negative situations."*
> **-Laura Hewitt**

Let's Not Get Serious

"Life is not a problem to be solved, but a reality to be experienced."
-Søren Kierkegaard

When learning how to give life the "right" kind of attention, the attention that will get you to the higher truth, it is pertinent to understand that taking things seriously will always become harmful. People take their clothing too seriously, their make-up, and the rest of their appearance way too seriously. We can take our social media presence or our conversations with friends and loved ones too seriously. What I see most often are people taking their jobs too seriously. They put their work above everything, and for obvious reasons, they believe that if they don't, they can lose everything they care about most. We take the moment too seriously, acting like 14 years of friendship doesn't matter because of a disagreement.

You see, seriously by definition elicits a feeling of rigidity we want to avoid. A "need" to have things a certain way, or else... Seriously means there can be a negative, often grave consequence on the other side. When we take things seriously and they don't go our way, it causes a certain level of unnecessary suffering. We feel like we lose control. Often, this alone can send some into a panic.

In the jungle, when trappers are trying to catch monkeys, they may use a simple and harmless trap that consists of a container and a piece of fruit. They cut a hole in the container, just big enough for the monkey to slip its hand inside. The fruit is placed inside and when the monkey reaches in to grab the fruit, together its fist and fruit become too big to pull out of the hole. This sends the monkey into a panic and the trapper can easily walk up and grab the monkey.

All the monkey needs to do is let go, but it feels like it *needs* the fruit. It *knows* it must to run, but it FEELS like it needs the fruit, and this creates a ton of anxiety. This tension, this tight grip on the way it SHOULD be, a preconceived expectation of reality, a want to have its cake and eat it too, a resistance against the inevitable, is what causes panic and ultimately gets the monkey caught.

Don't be a monkey.

Expectations will lead to suffering. It is basic human wiring to predict the future, but it is one of the greatest causes of suffering to become upset when things don't go the way we think they should have gone. As you walk through life's journey, loosen your grip on the way things *should* be. We may not always get what we want, and our expectations, our desires of the way things should be, are ingredients for disaster.

"Whether you think you can or think you can't, you're right."
-Henry Ford

The truth is that we don't actually know what we want. We think we do, but sometimes life has greater gifts in store. Often, I find myself and my clients riding out the storm only to see that there was something so much greater on the other side. I am a firm believer that we may not always get what we want, but we always have what we need.

Don't expect to be anywhere at any particular time with your healing and continue to practice the higher truth. You will get to exactly where you're growing.

There was a study done using elementary school students and teachers. After assessment, the names of the students with the five highest IQ's were given to the teachers. The teachers were told not to tell the students. At the end of the year, the five highest grades in the class belonged to the students whose names were given to the teachers. The amazing thing was that the names given to the teachers were random and not the highest IQ's in the class. Researchers guessed that the teachers' expectations of these students would yield these results, and they were right. The teachers' expectations created a beautiful, yet fabricated reality. They treated the students differently and the students proved the teachers' expectations right. Your expectations of where you should be in life, on how healthy you should feel at this point or how easy you believe something should be, will ultimately bring you distress.

Loosen your grip on how things *should* be.

If you want to experience life, you cannot grab onto it with force. Like swinging a golf club or playing the violin, a deliberate but loose grip will yield the best results. If you want to experience water, you cannot grab water. If you squeeze tightly you will lose it, but if you allow the water to run along your hand, you can truly experience it.

I am not telling you to throw all your cares to the wind. In fact, quite the opposite. Right now, your relationship with your family, your children, and most importantly the one with yourself will all dramatically improve when you start to take life **sincerely.**

Being sincere means approaching things with a genuine curiosity. With a full-of-care consideration. From now on, everything that you take so seriously, soften your grip, loosen the tension and approach it with a genuine curiosity. Think about your sleep, your timing, your appearance, your job, and anything else that NEEDS to go a certain way, or else... and write some of these below!

Things I Take Too Seriously:

_____

_____

_____

_____

Caring is sincere. You care about your child learning to drive, so you teach them everything you know. But when you worry, you are adding a level of need for control with circumstances that will always be outside of your reach. That is impractical and will bring you plenty of suffering. Worrying can be **selfish** too, in that it often requires the attention of others. At the core, worrying is caring with a thick layer of unnecessary fear and suffering.

Just as worrying can be selfish, neediness is the same. I *need* them to like me, I *need* her to be nice to me, I *need* him to hear me, I *need* to vent. As awful as this is going to sound, it is such a high truth: when you need something from someone else, when you need recognition, or you need someone to make you feel better, you are in a state of selfishness. There is nothing more selfish than taking from others to give to yourself. But, as you give more to yourself from yourself, as you continue following this process, as you become more self-sufficient, you are becoming a selfless human being. All that I teach is self-love. I know, this is one of the hardest parts to digest. I promise this is all for your greatest good.

Care more, be sincere, and stop taking life so seriously.

> *"If you suffer from anxiety because of your stressful life and your idea of everything needing to be "perfect" like I did, being a mom of 2 children, working a highly stressful and demanding job all while trying to pay a mountain of student loan debt, then Khail is who you're looking for! He has taught me more in a few months than my year of seeing a psychologist and therapists. I got my life back, no more panic attacks, I'm working a job that fits me and my lifestyle much more and I am happy! All because I put in the work to change. Check him out! Save your money and just invest in him!"*
> **-Vi Rodriguez**

Worrying versus Caring

To worry is to aggressively dream and practice
a reality that you hope never occurs.

Imagine you dreamt an amazing dream. The greatest dream of your life. You were rich. You were healthy. All your wildest desires were fulfilled in this dream. You had the car, the land, the house, the attention. You had it all.

Then you wake up. And you start telling everyone about this dream. Only, you aren't excited, but you are very upset. You say things like, "where's my Lamborghini? Where are my dancing party girls and my yacht? And just where the heck is Channing Tatum?"

Now imagine that everyone joins in. They all say things like "oh this is terrible! Why aren't all of these things here for you? I am so sorry! This is a travesty!"

Ridiculous right? Absolutely silly right?

Well this is worrying. This is exactly what worrying is. Worrying is fear and fear is **False Expectations Appearing Real.** It is a dream we come up with and is in no way true. It's worse than a dream. It's a daydream. It is a conscious dream (being fed by an old feeling). And we turn it into reality by focusing plenty of energy on it.

And it's crazy, because we share these worries with other people. And everyone joins in and empathizes with this make-believe scenario. Everyone is saying, "oh my gosh this is terrible, I hope you don't get fired! It's going to be okay, I know how hard this must be. It isn't fair that you have to go through this! And where's Channing Tatum??"

If they are positive friends, they may try to boost your self-esteem for you by giving you as many reasons why your fears are unwarranted, but rarely do we invalidate these concerns. We empathize with them, only encouraging the same self-harming behavior. We empathize because we believe our emotions are always warranted, but they are often rooted in misunderstanding. Our emotional state reflects what we've put into ourselves, how we experience and what we are feeding our minds. We are the orange.

If you start to see just how ludicrous worrying is, if you see it for what it really is, a self-defeating fear, a waste of time and energy, a guilt-driven program, you will start to manage your thoughts better and treat your life more responsibly.

Caring comes from a place of love. Caring is responsible. Caring about your child means reading books on parenting, or feeding them healthy foods, or showing them healthy attention and affection. Caring about your 16-year-old means showing them how to drive and helping them develop their skills

Worrying creates a space for fear and selfishness. It imposes your negative emotions onto others so that they feel them too. It clouds your judgement and takes away from your intelligence to make the best decisions possible because that is what happens to your brain when it is scared versus when it is happy. This is why we are irrational when we are afraid or angry.

Worrying adds a layer of stress and guilt to the situation. Often the things you worry most about are the last things you want to add an extra layer of stress or guilt to. They're usually the last places you would want to be selfish.

And remember how the mind works. When you worry, you are seeking to have an intention of everything you truly don't want to go wrong. Worrying about a car accident is applying the attention to intend to worry more about car accidents. Do you understand? This is tough for people to grasp. Worrying is easy and feels hard. Caring is hard but feels so good. It takes strength to avoid worrying. Strength you certainly have and will continue to grow.

> *"Let your bending in the archer's hand be for gladness; For even as He loves the arrow that flies, so He loves also the bow that is stable."*
> -Kahlil Gibran

In his poem "Your Children", Kahlil Gibran talks about the strength in flexibility of the bow that is the parent, being bent by life's circumstances. The more flexible, the more loving, the stronger, the further and straighter the arrow (your child) will fly.

To beat worrying, start interrupting your negative pattern of worrying and replace it with love. Ask yourself, if I were approaching this test, this job interview, this conversation from a place of love, how would it look?

It might look something like this: I would love this position because I will be a great asset to this company. I love the opportunity to interview. I love that these humans would take time out of their busy day to meet with me. With love, I am here to spread joy and smiles. I'll see if I can make them smile while I am there. I'll look for a genuine way to connect with them.

Approach your life with calm care and leave worrying behind.

Love is abundant. Fear is lacking. Love is complete. Fear is empty. Love is excitement, curiosity and enthusiasm. Fear is hindering, limiting and protecting. Which are you practicing?

As you begin to care more and worry less, you are going to run into the silliest problem of all: realizing you are worried because there's nothing to worry about. This is normal, and it too shall pass.

What are some of your typical worries? Write them down and begin to loosen your grip on these. Decide how you can shift from worry to care and make a conscious effort to do so regularly!

My Worries

_____

_____

_____

_____

_____

_____

_____

_____

_____

_____

> "I was struggling severely with anxiety and panic attacks for about 6 months. I had to quit my job of 5 years, just thinking about driving would give me panic. This grew into health and social anxiety. I was avoiding grocery stores, restaurants and birthday parties. The anxiety and guilt were debilitating. Zoloft helped a little but I was still battling every day. After speaking with Khail, I KNEW that he was the perfect person to help. I am now driving again, going to public places, and enroll my daughters in dance classes! I have the tools I need to overcome any obstacle that comes at me in life whether it be anxiety, stress, or hardship. If you are struggling, if you feel like you've hit rock bottom- that this is your "life" now.... please reach out to Khail! I can't say enough good things about him and his program!"
> **-Akira Bourgeois**

Bonus #3: Growth Mindset Mastery

This is fantastic! You're up to your 3rd bonus practice! Celebrate! This one is going to change everything for you. From now on, when something you judge as "bad" happens to you in your life, I want you to begin to react to it differently. The first thing I want you to do is smile, laugh, and say "this is a good thing". Why?

"Everything is happening for me!" If you believe in a higher power, you know this to be true, but you may not always align yourself with it. If you want growth, you need to understand that you are getting everything you need to grow! Realistically, logically, when something feels bad, it is telling you that you have room for growth. Your enemies are your greatest teachers. Start looking for how to learn, accepting things as they come, reacting peacefully, and moving past suffering as quickly as possible. You will gain wisdom very quickly with this mindset. Everything truly is happening for you. Today's pain may very well be tomorrow's blessing.

"Khail has helped me change my state of mind. I was struggling with anxiety/depression, I was stuck in that state of panic all day. I couldn't drive far out, I couldn't stay home by myself, I took a leave of absence from work. I was in a really dark place. But, ONE phone call with Khail I am in such a better place! Seriously, a week after we spoke I drove out further than I normally would, I am staying home by myself, I picked a date to return back to work. I am living the life I had before anxiety/depression hit. I am so happy! Words cannot express the appreciation I have for Khail. His system works! Thank you Khail, you saved my life. I said it once, and I will say it again, you are Heaven sent!"
-Stephanie Mclaughlin

Why Seek a Higher Truth?

What you love empowers you. What you fear disempowers you.

Flash back to that person tailgating you that you sent lovingly on their way. Why on earth should you send them love and positivity? Why not give them what they "deserve"?

As I mentioned earlier, the subconscious mind is like a farm that we are consciously and unconsciously cultivating. Every thought, feeling, bit of information is a seed. Remember the orange analogy as it relates to what we put into ourselves. Also, keep in mind that we are consciously aware of only a fraction of a percent of all that the mind takes in. Remember the study with the money? Where the lucky people had wired their minds to see what the unlucky could not?

You see, the way you choose to experience will ultimately define the way you experience life going forward. If you are constantly fighting, you will see more opportunity to fight. But, if you are regularly seeking the higher truth, spreading love and positivity, seeking ways to feel calm, your subconscious mind will tailor your experience for more of that.

Sounds too good to be true right? Remember your mind is taking in 400 billion bits of information every second. That's a lot of experience we are missing. There are silver linings to nearly every poor experience. How are you supposed to experience them without seeking the higher truth? It won't happen! Your mind may instantly combat this, thinking of the worst experience imaginable, so that you can discredit this silver lining. But your mind is filtered! Even what you may deem as terrible, someone with a positive or growth-filter in their mind may see some purpose or beauty. Time is a wonderful teacher. You just never know how things will wind up.

It is time to reflect on those same old songs you play for yourself. The negative talk tracks you are mixing up in your mind. It is time to rewrite the music. As an exercise, I want you to put a positive spin, seek a silver lining, or focus on the good as it relates to those same old songs after some more explanation.

If you think you are stupid, it is time to say I am becoming smarter every day. I love to learn. I am life's student. I love to grow.

If you're afraid something terrible is going to happen, it is time to start enjoying the good that exists. List what and why it is more important to focus on what is here. It is time to start imagining positive outcomes! What if this is the greatest experience of my life?

Remember, anxiety is taking the negative in your life and manifesting it as horrible physical symptoms, panic attacks and intrusive thoughts. All the negative in your life is very primal to your brain. The mind will relate negativity to a tiger trying to eat you. **Negativity turns to fear.**

This process isn't just a reactionary approach. I don't necessarily believe in reacting to situations based on the problem at hand. What we are doing with this program is using a proactive approach to bring you a happier, calmer, and more positive life. You are taking steps towards becoming a better, stronger, calmer, more anxiety-resistant version of you!

Perhaps you are happy right now, and anxiety is just in the way. Well, there are a few common side-effects to being even happier I'd love to discuss.

First, when you are happier, you are about 30% more intelligent. That's why when I describe the Pause Breath, I say that thinking of a box of kittens is a good enough start. Why be neutral? When you are taking a test, or putting your skills to the test, do you do better relaxed or anxious? You may believe that stress helps, but it is only because fear has been a driver in your life for so long. It is not necessary to be stressed in order to get things done.

The longest research study in history has been going on for over 75 years. The study is testing for the top contributors of health and longevity in people's lives. Researchers found that happiness, above genes, diet, location, financial status and every other thing you can think of, is the most important factor when creating a longer and healthier life. Happiness!

How is that possible? Because there's more to it than just feeling good. Those good feelings are good chemicals, but its more than that! It is all about what a happy mindset does for your body, your path in life, your choices and the attitude that keeps you going! Your reality can be filtered through a mindset that seeks pleasure or pain.

So, learning to let go, feeding the good wolf, planting crops instead of craps, and seeking the higher truth will not only help you eliminate anxiety (and most, if not all suffering in your life), but it will help you to live your life to its maximum potential!

Rewrite your music, those same old songs in your head, so that it becomes something beautiful enough that you would share it with those you care most about. Reframe the negative thoughts in your mind to be something you would read to yourself as a child. Take some time on this. This is a skill you will want to use every day for the rest of your life. Here's an example: "I hope I don't have a panic attack". Now you could reframe this to say, "I am taking action for my health", "I can see a light at the end of the tunnel and I am growing towards it", or **the best way to do it is to talk about what you DO want,** "I love enjoying time with my family, being free and silly, and spending time on my passion projects!"

Rewritten Songs

_____

_____

_____

_____

_____

_____

_____

_____

_____

_____

_____

_____

_____

_____

_____

> *"Khail Kapp knows how to handle anxiety and he works with you to pull out your potential. He is full of rewarding advice and really has a handle on life. I highly recommend giving him a chance. The results are phenomenal. I have been in therapy and on SSI for almost 10 years. After two weeks of working with Khail, I have no depression, I applied for online college to get a degree in psychology, and I have very minimal anxiety which Khail helps me eliminate. He changes lives."*
> **-Brittany Gunderson**

Here's a line that follows you in life. You can step over it anytime.
On one side there's suffering.

On the other is the higher truth

Attention Deep Dive

"Change happens when the pain of staying the same is greater than the pain of change."
-Tony Robbins

By now, you may understand that changing your perspectives can drastically change your experience. But what if the thing you are experiencing on the outside doesn't seem to change? Or what if you still believe that changing your perspective may not change anything outside of you? You may still be on the fence at this point.

If you are thinking the world is judging you and you walk into a coffee shop, your subconscious mind will help you see faces as judgmental. You take a glance as definitive proof that someone doesn't like you or something of that nature. If I took a random picture of a you at a given time of the day, would that represent your opinions? Would a random facial expression, perhaps one that is made when you're holding back a burp or when a smell reminds you of a childhood memory, would these facial expressions be a good representation of who you are? Of course not. I often catch myself making dramatic faces when opening a jar or stretching out some soreness. If someone sees me when I'm doing this, they would probably think that my appendix is about to explode. We are all guilty of playing this detective game, assuming we know what the world is thinking. But if you choose to see the world as loving, you will notice a child playing, a puppy wiggling, or someone displaying kindness.

Life is one giant scavenger hunt. We are always looking for something. Our inner-dialog is our GPS.

Keeping in mind that the brain only absorbs, if I ask you not to think of an elephant, you can't do anything but think of that elephant. You bring into your reality whatever you do want to think about, just as easily as what you don't want to think about. You're thinking about both things, you see? Your mind doesn't understand "no". The answer is always yes. "I want to find Waldo", "I'd love to find money on the ground", or "where's the hottie at this party" all translates to "these things are important to me. Seek more." "I hate anxiety" translates to "anxiety is important to me... Seek more!" Seek more reasons, triggers, proof, more opportunities to talk about anxiety, are all viable subconscious translations of "I hate anxiety."

If you are replaying a bad memory or a fear again and again, you will feel and experience that again and again. You are practicing and therefor hardwiring the subconscious mind. You are telling your body that experiencing this fear is important to you, and the body will program for it. The program will ensure you experience it regularly, find a ton of research on exactly why you should experience that, and perpetuate anything that will continue to feed into that negative experience. This ability to find the research you are *intending* to find is called a "confirmation bias". The mind is powerful at finding exactly what you are *feeling* for. So, if you hate panic, your intention is fearing panic and seeking more of it. That fear translates to things like "this is hopeless" and "I've got to run away from this." Then, through a confirmation bias, all that you seek will confirm this intention. The studies that will pop out at you will validate your concerns, digging you an even deeper hole. This is why attention is so important in rewiring your belief system and sending you on a proper course.

The only way to begin to experience life differently is to rewire your mind for the experiences that you want to have. We must change your beliefs!

When researchers are testing new drugs, they will often give patients useless pills filled with sugar or starch and pretend they are the real medication. With zero medicinal properties, one would expect that the pills would have no effect. And they test the fake pills (placebos) against the real medication to show that the real medication is doing its job.

What they don't usually talk about are the effects of placebos. The placebo effect is readily published. Patients get better from taking fake pills. In fact, a significant number of patients get better from the placebo effect! Because they **believe** that they are taking real medication, because they trust the doctor more than anyone, and because they believe that "this is it", they've finally found the thing to help, because of these things, their belief system creates the healing changes in their bodies.

This works the other way as well. Why does a medication work for someone and not for another? Often, it can be said that it is because that patient doesn't believe they can get any healthier. But, a better way to hear this is that the patients were not **ready** to be healed.

Are you ready to be healed?

Sometimes, we hold onto suffering because we feel like we deserve it. Sometimes it is because we want others to empathize with that pain. Much like our caveman Bob shared about the tiger, misery loves company. Above everything, we resist change because subconsciously, change could mean danger or death. Any change. And you will find yourself questioning whether it is even in your best interests to create a new version of you, as silly as that sounds, because you can easily fool yourself by empathizing with your feelings of discomfort toward change. I often see people confidently affirming that they're ready to be well. Let's be real here. Who wouldn't affirm this? Obviously, everyone believes they're ready. So slow down for a second. If it seems too obvious, your ego is blocking you from truth. If everyone thinks they're ready, and being read is an important part, why don't more people get better? Validation. Addiction to fear. Longing for empathy and the *need* for the pity of others. We are going to break this sneaky belief inside of you.

You are worthy of anything you can imagine. You're worthy of happiness.

There have been countless studies on placebo effects for surgeries as well. As a medical device rep, I regularly consulted during knee surgeries. Standing behind surgeons during the operation, guiding them on the proper use of my equipment, and trouble-shooting any difficulties was the bulk of my career for about 5 years. Every so often, surgeons would have a patient's family approve a fake surgery. The surgery would be staged as a real procedure. The patient would be prepped, put under, and the doctor would make incisions. After taking a few pictures with the arthroscope (a camera on the end of something the size of a straw) of the inside of the joint to prove that the patient had the disease/issue, the surgeon would stitch close up the patient and tell them it was a success.

Many patients reported full recoveries because they believed their ailment was cured. Even more miraculous, something like cartilage, the smooth surfaces in our joints, a material we are supposedly only able to grow so much of as children, and according it modern medicine, "unable" to regenerate, has been proven to regenerate from these placebo surgeries. So, a doctor pretends to perform a meniscus repair or cartilage replacement, and the patient goes back to playing sports in a few weeks with a healthy knee!

How? Why? Because the human body is intelligent. It is capable of more than we can access at any given moment. Tell me, do you know how to grow teeth? What about taking stem cells and turning them into heart cells? Consider yourself lucky. If we had access to this intelligence at all times, we would have all disintegrated ourselves a thousand times over with every "meltdown" we've experienced.

Bottom line: if patients can regrow cartilage, repair traumatic brain injuries, or recover from paralysis, you can eliminate your constant anxiety, panic attacks, depression, PTSD, insomnia, fibromyalgia, or anything you put your mind to!

What do you believe? And what do you want to believe? In the spaces below, write down some of your current beliefs as they relate to this journey. Are these beliefs "limiting" you from experiencing a better life? Next to the current limiting beliefs, reframe them for a world you would prefer to experience, a reality you want to live. You may *want* to believe you can get better, but even with all that you've learned and the testimonials, you still find it hard. Be honest! We will get deeper and more involved as this book goes on.

Beliefs and Reframing Limiting Beliefs

_____

_____

_____

_____

_____

_____

_____

_____

_____

_____

_____

_____

_____

_____

"I suffered from anxiety for about 15 years. After talking to Khail, all I can say is "WOW". He was able to walk me through an airport mid-panic! I'm using his techniques on the regular now. I am able to train my brain and keep anxiety under control. Khail is amazing. He absolutely knows what he's talking about with anxiety, depression, panic and all that. I decide whether I have a good day or a bad day now. I am so blessed that I was scrolling through Facebook and met Khail."
-Jenny Coleman

Questions

"Ask and you will receive. Knock and it will be opened for you."
-Matthew 7:7

Why do I have anxiety? Why me? Why did this happen? Why does my heart flutter when I see news headlines about car crashes? Why do I get dizzy when I stand up? Why can't I leave the house anymore? Why do I have symptoms out of nowhere? Is this normal? Has anyone else felt this way? Is this hereditary? Why do I panic when I....?

Sound familiar? The question "why" is an endless rabbit hole you do not want to fall into. You may start with good intentions, but it is a trap that the ego, the subconscious mind, loves to lure you into. It loves it because it freezes you. A big problem with reactional therapies is that they give answers to these questions. Then you're left with the feeling of "what now?" What are you supposed to do with the answers to these? If someone tells you that you have anxiety because of your childhood, great! What now? You can't get a new childhood. You can't even have an old childhood either because it is already gone. The past doesn't exist. Only your attention and your practiced feelings towards it exist. If someone tells you that your anxiety is a result of medication, an illness, or anything outside of you, great! It isn't your fault. Ah yes, now you can lay back and rest easy... Wait, no you can't. You still have anxiety symptoms.

Someone once asked me, "Khail, my psychiatrist is a jerk! They told me to stop talking about my past and start talking about my future. What should I do?" And for the first time ever, I gave medical advice, and told them "stay with that therapist!" Why? Because there's only so much you can know about your past. Only so many dots you can connect and only so many patterns you will find. You will talk yourself into a corner again and again. I find that many therapies work because patients get sick of telling the same old story!

Perhaps you feel guilty all the time because your mother felt it and used it to drive you to do better. Great! Now what? See, the patterns in your life right now have been there for some time. Anything you're carrying from the past, you're displaying right now.

I believe that continuously rehashing the past can only be helpful when one decides that they are sick of telling that story, and they start to tell another. Please, share your story. Don't carry this burden alone. But once you do, if it doesn't serve you, let it go. If it can't inspire others and it is only bringing you pain, please let it go! I'll explain more on how to do this soon, and as you continue with the foundational practices, this will get easier.

For now, avoid the "why" monster and focus on asking "what" to do right now to take a step forward! Be on the lookout for loops of questions that only perpetuate the multi-tasking, overthinking, unaccepting monster that is anxiety. Keep it simple. **Stick with this program for 4 weeks minimum and then check in to see if you've grown.** Many suffering this way continue to ask questions and seek short-term gains and easy solutions, but not you! You're here to create long-lasting growth!

NOTE: Have you started writing in your Brag Book yet? Keep up with your accomplishments!

> *"After 6 years of agoraphobia, I am back to work and thriving! I haven't had a panic attack since starting Khail's program. I was even faced with an insane storm while the tornado sirens went off for 15 mins! I felt myself panic and got that good old depersonalization going for a moment, but I was able to reverse it thanks to the tools Khail has taught me!"*
> **-Rebecca Roberts**

Accepting and Letting Go

"Tension is who you think you should be. Relaxation is who you are."
-Chinese Proverb

I've coached people that have tried acceptance therapy. I believe that the main reason the majority that don't succeed from trying therapies like this are because they are lacking the foundational practices you have been working on. If you are reading this book straight through, here's just another reminder to stick with the foundation! It changes your nervous system and beliefs from the inside out. It is like laying one brick at a time. So, as we dive into acceptance, allow yourself to hear this with a fresh set of ears. Now, allow me to tell you my favorite story.

Once there lived a farmer who was tending to his prized horse on a windy morning. The wind blew the horse's gate opened and the horse took off into the wild.

The local villagers heard what happened and rushed to the farm. They exclaimed, "Oh no! Your best horse ran away! That's terrible!" To which the farmer replied, "maybe."

The next day, the horse returned! And he brought with him 3 gorgeous wild horses. The villagers heard the news and rushed to the farm. "This is wonderful!", they exclaimed. To which the farmer replied, "maybe".

The following day, the farmer's son was attempting to tame one of the horses when he was violently thrown off. The young man shattered his leg. Hearing the news and clearly having way too much time on their hands, the villagers rushed to the farm. "Your poor son, those awful horses, this is terrible!", they cried. To which the farmer replied, "maybe".

The next morning, a loud knock at the door shook the farmer awake. Upon opening the door, he was greeted by some men from the army. They were there to recruit his son, but after inspecting the young man's condition, deemed him not fit for war, and bid the farmer and his son farewell.

The villagers rushed to the farmers house after seeing the soldiers leave. "Your son did not get drafted because of his injury? How lucky!" they exclaimed. To which the farmer replied, "maybe"...

Ah it's amazing! This tale is powerful! I love it so much because that stoic farmer just *gets it*. It isn't easy to get. It is very difficult not to get fixated on a small window of time due to our judgments and predispositions. But it is very possible and incredibly rewarding! You don't need to practice stoicism either. You can do all of this with love!

Life is like a wave. Whether you are surfing the crest or riding down in the trough, it is all choice. It's all about perspective.

Sometimes things can seem like they are in our way: a traffic jam or someone getting sick. Sometimes "horrible and unfortunate" things happen like the abuse I experienced as a child. But, if we get lost in the moment, if we are focusing on the negative as it appears in the present, we may miss our opportunity to experience the good that is existing simultaneously. We may miss the opportunities that can come from what is currently seen as a misfortune. If I still suffered from the abuse I experienced, you would not be reading this book. On the other hand, had I not experienced that abuse, you would not be reading this book.

I've experienced this phenomenon countless times. I am late to a meeting only to discover everyone else is too. I get sick and my work is delayed yet everything works out amazingly. Perhaps you get fired from a job, only to wind up getting a much better job down the road.

Keep your chin up and your perspective optimistic, and you will be sure to get to where ever it is you are growing!

There is an old tale of two monks standing at a rivers edge. Before crossing the raging river, the older monk notices a beautiful woman walking towards him. He immediately diverts his attention away.

The younger monk smiles at the lovely damsel as she requests assistance across the river. Knowing the current was too strong for her, and obviously delighted to help such a beautiful woman, the young monk invited her to climb on his back.

The three crossed the river, the woman thanked the monks and went on her way. Nearly 8 hours had passed and the older monk, showing signs of extreme agitation, but the monks kept on their journey. This agitation led the older monk to anger, and he couldn't sleep. Tossing and turning all night, the older monk was beside himself with rage the next morning. When the younger monk awoke, he immediately lashed out at him.

"I can't believe you did that", he said. Surprised, the younger monk asked him what he was referring to and the older monk replied, "You know what you did! I can't believe you would just carry that beautiful woman across the river like that! We are celibate monks after all!"

The younger monk surprised, turned to the older monk with a smile and responded "I put her down hours ago, and here you are still carrying her."

In life, we have the ability to let go or to carry what is most important to us. What we give repeated attention to, the subconscious loops on repeat, ensuring we don't forget it. So, as negative thoughts come to you, it's up to you to simply breathe and let them go, by choosing to grab onto something worth holding.

Breathe, and choose what you would rather hold onto.

Be like the young monk here and when life throws you something you don't wish to experience, make the most of it, and when it is done, do a Pause Breath, let it go, and focus on the journey at hand. It takes practice. It takes the desire to be happy over the *need* to prove something. How many sleepless nights have you had? How many fights and broken relationships have you experienced? Life is short. Focus on what you truly wish to experience and allow others to be themselves.

The easiest way to put something down is to pick something else up.

> "I was first introduced to Khail's program while pregnant with twins. I didn't really think of my problems as if they were anxiety. I struggled with anger, couldn't let things go, was depressed and had a lot of negativity in my life. After just a few weeks, I'm more peaceful, happier and more content than I have ever been before! I have so much hope for where I will be in the future. Khail's coaching program has given me everything I need to get to where I want to be, and I do recommend his program to everyone I know because even if you don't struggle with anxiety or anything obvious, this program will help you have the life you've always wanted to have!"
> **-Esther Godfrey**

Life's Ups and Downs

When you listen to music, when you dance, when you sing, when you play, the point isn't to get to the end. It is to enjoy the experience along the way. So, it is with life.

Along this journey, there will be trials. One day you may think you have mastered this entire process, only to feel like you're back at square one. This isn't true. Once you've begun this process, **there are no mistakes**. Everything is exactly as it should be. If it wasn't, it wouldn't be. The deeper understanding here is that if you have a bad day, it serves a purpose.

Your bad day is giving you a realistic environment to test your new skills or it is showing you that you still have growth.

Don't be discouraged by growth! This is having a fixed mindset. Letting the idea of growth discourage you would only make logical sense if you feel like you've already arrived. But if you've already arrived, why do you still suffer? If you were perfect, then I could understand the confusion. Don't seek arrival. Don't seek completion.

Seek measurable results, no matter how small.

Imagine being a rocket scientist, having devoted your entire life to a project, only to watch it explode right in front of you. And I mean imagine every waking moment of your life leading up to a failure like that! Millions upon millions of dollars, countless man hours of perfecting something only to watch it disappear in an instant. Now imagine it happened twice.

Oh, one more thing: imagine that you are creating this company from scratch and the whole world is watching. This is the story of Elon Musk and SpaceX. Since his first "failures" they have launched 53 successful missions and completely redefined space travel.

But that's Elon Musk, Khail. I'm no Elon Musk. Oh, but you are. You see, chances are that when you were learning to walk, you fell, hard, hundreds of times. And your parents, like most, weren't trying to immediately stand you back up. In all actuality they probably held you, felt terrible for 30 minutes and hoped that if you tried again soon, you would magically be successful.

As a child, the thought of quitting never even enters our minds. Not once does an infant look at the ground and say to herself, "this is impossible, walking is not for me." You don't see people crawling around all over the world just saying, "oh, walking? Yeah, I can't do that. I tried! But it just isn't something I'll ever be able to do."

See we learn to fear failure. From our society, from our school systems, and from our upbringing. We fear embarrassment. We see trials and the journey as daunting and it clouds our understanding that we are, in fact, LIMITLESS. That if we put our minds to something, we will accomplish it. That trials are part of the journey and that everything we don't like is a stepping stone towards mastery.

We are human. Not, we are *only* human. This is the silliest saying I hear: "I'm only human." As opposed to what? What on earth are we comparing ourselves to by limiting ourselves with such a phrase?

We are human! We carve mountains, travel to space, cure diseases. We are all the same creature with a powerful brain! The most powerful system in the universe in fact. Don't give up because you have one hard minute, or a crazy hour, or a rough day or two. Why give up ever? If you believe in something, NEVER give up. *But Khail, I've suffered for 176 years now...* Your healing, that light at the end of the tunnel, is well worth this journey, I assure you. You will be more present, more grateful, take less for granted, wiser, happier and more loving! This process of improvement is a journey. It is going to take weeks, and that's okay! Right? Give me a "heck yes!"

Write a note for yourself. Post it on the bathroom mirror or leave it on your dashboard, or somewhere you will read it every day. Tell yourself that this process is a journey, to stick with it, and remember not to take life so seriously! I love seeing pictures of your notes, so please share them with me on Facebook!

The next point to understand is that nothing will ever go 100% your way, but that is a good thing. It's a magical thing in fact. If you were in 100% control of everything around you, life would get dull very quickly. There needs to be contrast. You need to have different opinions and personalities around you. It is how ideas move forward. It is the only true way you can define yourself. By seeing the differences in others, you define yourself. And above everything, it keeps life interesting.

See the beauty in the contrast. If you have a significant other and wish they were more like you, understand that this is a whole person. They have lived an infinite number of experiences from an entirely different perspective. Even if you've shared the same external space with them, a slight variation in their wiring can mean an endless supply of different opinions. Honestly, imagine living with you. Just you. You'd kill the other version of yourself in about 4 hours. Love others for what they are AND what they aren't.

Choose to see life's ups and downs as part of the masterpiece and you will surely master peace.

Everything You Don't Like is Good

I have spent years seeking the ideal place, only to realize I must be it.

Change is hard. If it were easy, we would all be billionaires, have chiseled bods and living happily ever after on our own individual islands. I know how cliché it is to even describe this, but it is very important to dive into this lesson.

Some lessons will feel funny along this path. Some will seem wrong, impossible, or just irrelevant. What you must remember is cognitive dissonance. You must consider that right now, your mind and your body only care about your survival, and that **any change feels like a threat towards your very existence**. It sounds dramatic, but it's true.

Since you're alive right now, the majority of who you are doesn't want you to change anything. The way you brush your teeth, the way you climb out of bed, the way you perceive or react, what you believe, all these things need to remain exactly as they are or even lessen and become safer, according to your mind and body.

Any deviation from this could mean death. Not really. Not in actuality, but your subconscious doesn't know this.

Everyone that I coach will come back after a lesson and say something like, "yes I understand Khail, but it's hard." Well good! **The harder it is for you to do, the bigger the opportunity for growth is.** If I wanted to eat 45 hot dogs in 30 minutes, it would be really really hard. Because I can probably only eat 4 or 5 hot dogs before I throw up with my current mindset, stomach expansion and relaxation capabilities, and technique. But that doesn't mean it is impossible. It only means I have about 40 hotdogs worth of growth ahead of me. It only means I have work to do. And giving attention to anything else, is an excuse, and will only help to hold me back. If I constantly focus on how hard it is, it is going to be hard, and it is going to get harder. But, if I focus on my upside potential, I will only climb.

If you are suffering from a body that regularly experiences anxiety, one would assume that you have significant growth to experience before you feel calm, before you can focus on something for a few minutes, before you can fall asleep rather quickly.

So, when you're trying to put your phone down, when you're trying to sit still or sit quietly without NEEDING to break the silence, when you're trying to tolerate certain people or even keep your attention on this book, and you find it hard... good. This "hardness" is for you to see your room for growth, where to grow, and then to watch your progress. As it gets easier, you're getting better!

The difficulty deserves your gratitude. It is teaching you inner-peace.

You are trying to get better. From another perspective, you can say that you are trying NOT to be a certain way anymore. Maybe that way is foggy or absent minded. Maybe you don't want to be so irritable. Maybe you are tired of having awful anxiety symptoms. Whatever it is that you are trying to get away from, you need to adopt a different perspective.

You must be on the lookout for anything you don't like in your life. You might be sitting there thinking, "Khail, this is easy. I know what I don't like. I hate it." Sure. And hating it is part of the problem.

Hate is your prison, but love is your salvation.

If you were a detective, you wouldn't hate every clue that helped you solve a mystery. I'm just imagining this neurotic detective yelling, "NOOOOOOO!" every time she found another clue. I digress. Every clue, every tip, every bad thing you can find about yourself that you want gone, will help you get one step closer to becoming the person you want to be. One step closer to happy. One step closer to calm. One step closer to unshakable peace!

So, you need to take on the role of detective here. You are no victim. You are a perceptive sleuth ready to uncover every bit of wrong with your life. Every time you see or feel something negative, it is time to celebrate!

If life felt perfect, then you wouldn't have any symptoms. There would be no clues for you to sniff out. But, since you have some growth to work on, these clues are going to help you get to where you are growing. Be eager to see them, not hurt by them. Every time your belly feels off, great! Take a slow deep breath and think positive. Every time you get a little dizzy, excellent! Pause and breathe, then tell yourself that you are healthy. Every time you find a negative thought, fantastic! Pause Breath that thought and think loving, happy thoughts.

A great way to begin to shift into a growth mindset is responding to every one of life's hiccups with enthusiasm immediately. Say "I'm excited!" or "I love this!" as your first response, and watch your new perspective open up an entirely different path. Sound crazy? Well, chemically speaking, fear and excitement are the same thing!

Do you see how this relates to the way your subconscious is wired? If you want to feel good, as you walk through the garden of life, you need to pause at the weeds, and plant flowers. Currently, everything you don't like about your life, you need to notice. At this point, you are probably pretty good at this skill. Maybe even too good.

But then you must be happy to find it, and even happier to replace it with something positive. Use your Pause Breath to interrupt the old pattern, and know that if you are constantly finding weeds, your garden will surely be beautiful by the time you are done with this work.

You see, when something doesn't feel right, a person upsets you or you realize you are growing impatient, whatever it is, it is telling you that you have room for growth. You must change if you are to better handle yourself in the future. Everything you don't like right now is a good thing. It is a signal to help you get better. You've got this!

And remember, don't take anything too seriously.

As an awesome exercise, briefly describe a few recent challenges you've experienced. To warm up your new perspective, imagine that you handled them with a growth mindset. Write the challenges and then imagine yourself reacting excited, and taking a step towards seeking a lesson, rather than pity or validation. This brief exercise can be done after every poor experience to get you closer towards the limitless individual that you most certainly are!

_____

_____

_____

_____

_____

_____

_____

_____

_____

_____

> *"My divorce made me realize that all of my self-worth had been put into this man. Enter my brother, Khail Kapp, whose teaching and coaching have made me see that the real me is beautiful and worthy of love and kindness. I am learning to see that the glass is half full, and that there is still a life in front of me no matter my age."*
> **-Heather Felton**

Just Who Do You Think You Are?

"I am not who you think I am. I am not who I think I am. I am who I think you think I am."
-Thomas Cooley

At this point of learning mindfulness, practicing presence and seeing which wolf you're feeding, you might be feeling a bit at odds with yourself. Perhaps you really resonated with the part about cognitive dissonance and you are feeling like there are two of you at war.

But how can there be two of you? There is only one you. This other you that you feel, this is not you. But who could it be?

Who are you? If you think left turn while driving, you can make your car turn left, but you are not your car. You're obviously not your clothes. I suppose you can't be your hair or nails. If you lost your left hand, it might be difficult to manage for a while, especially if you're a lefty, but you would manage. So, you aren't your hand. Then, I suppose you aren't your body either.

Essentially, you cannot be anything that can be added to. This body is just pieces of earth material that put itself together. Bananas, pizza, salad, chocolate... These things are not you. They've just helped create a body for you. So, who are you?

You are your personality, right? But, what if you're sad? What if you're very angry? What if you haven't slept? What if you lost someone close to you? What if you win the lottery? Are you now someone else? Do you get to pick and choose who you are? Don't answer that last one yet.

If your mood can change who you are, so to speak, how can you be your personality? A personality is confining. It is merely habits of thoughts, behaviors and emotions that are created by nature and nurture. Your personality is just a product of what your parents gave you and how you've experienced life up until this point. But it also has so much to do with what you are experiencing right now. Your job. The music you listen to. The media you surround yourself with. Your friends and family, the culture you're in and society. All these things are playing a role. But it is mostly a subconscious role.

Let's try an exercise you should be becoming very good at by now. Do the Pause Breath for a moment and bring yourself to a happy state.

After doing this, you are like a different person. Whatever reason that got you here reading my work right now didn't exist for a moment there. This defining characteristic didn't exist. Just like that, you're different because your state of being is different. If you skipped that Pause Breath, go ahead and do it now. I swear I will turn this book right around if you don't start doing for you!

A personality is simply the lens through which we see the world; a loudspeaker through which we communicate. It's also the membrane through which we absorb experience around us. It serves a purpose, but it is not permanent. And it is a very rigid construct. It is limiting. It labels you. So, why not choose to create a lens that works for you? Why confine yourself to such a strict box? Why confine yourself at all? Why keep anything you do not like?

> *"You are under no obligation to be the same person*
> *you were five minutes ago"*
> -Alan Watts

As you're mastering the Pause Breath technique, you can relate to this idea, even if only briefly. If you aren't there yet, you will be. Once you begin to taste this clarity, you will realize that the you that you think you are is merely a loose mask. An old habit.

So, who are you? You are something deeper. You are something much more than a personality could simply define. You are not your thoughts, but the observer of them. You are not your personality, for this is the boat. **You are the captain.** You do not need to identify yourself with your material items, your body, personality or even your thoughts and feelings. These things are not you, they are yours.

You are sitting there thinking that it makes sense, but it is hard. Remember the dissonance you will feel. This war, this you versus the old self, this is a war between you and the **ego**. The ego is a conglomerate of your personality and the conditions and experiences that create your state of being. The ego is your journey. The ego is not good or bad, but it *is* limiting. And the ego very much likes to play like it is you. But it isn't. You aren't the ego. You are limitless, beyond flexible, ever-changing and ever-evolving.

You are your choices in every moment. You are whatever you want to be.

When you watch a speed boat in the water, it leaves behind a wake. As you watch the wake, it eventually fades into the rest of the waves. If you splash the wake, throw rocks at the wake, surf the wake, you will not change the trajectory of the boat. The boat is not controlled by the wake. Like this, you are not controlled by your past. Only your attention to the past will keep you there, just as staring at the wake behind the boat will not make for an accurate or even safe journey!

The same goes for the present. If you do not like your current circumstances, you need only to shift your attention slightly to have a different experience. **Set your gaze**

for where you are going. If you are in a bad place, where do you want to be? Like piloting a boat, you need to keep your attention fixated on where you want to go, rather than where you came from or where you currently are. If you were in a boat, paying attention to the wake, you would surely lose control. This is life. Do you see it in your life? Do you see how getting stuck in one place or constantly focusing on your negative past is spinning you out of control?

Below, describe some areas of your life where you may be staring at the wake. Getting this on paper is important! Even if it is something recent, it's the wake, and it's spinning you out of control! Use the last line to define where you are going to focus your gaze from now on!

Hint: you're going to focus on your growth, a 2.0 version of you, your happiness, etc.

_____

_____

_____

_____

_____

_____

_____

_____

The ego has defined a constricting little box to keep you in. It did this for your safety and survival. Without a conscious captain at the wheel of the boat, we may steer off course. But you are now becoming more conscious every day! Your mindfulness practices are taking the captain's responsibilities back as the weeks go on. This may scare the ego. It may feel very uncomfortable. But if you persist, you will change the mind into a place worth living.

As an exercise, define your current personality. If you would like to understand more about your current state, check out the Myers-Briggs personality test. I find this to be the best judge of this mask we define ourselves by. You can do a quick Google search and take the test for free. Use these constricting labels to better understand where you want to be, what areas you can change to get better, and what areas are empowering your current state.

My personality type is:_____

My stressors are:

_____

_____

_____

Your *stressors* are the boundaries of the box a personality confines you to. How will you break free? Answer: by seeing them and changing your perspective.

> *"Thank the universe for Khail! Have anxiety? Khail is your man! Not only did his step by step program help me to understand and eliminate my anxiety, but I learnt so many things about myself that I'd previously overlooked! This self-discovery certainly improved my way of thinking within. My days seem to shine brighter and the weight has lifted off my shoulders where I finally feel like I can breathe without fear or worry. It is not only his program, but his support he offers you with compassion, empathy and understanding. I highly recommend Khail and his program if you are ready to live a happier life without anxiety. Thank you Khail for changing my life."*
> **-Naomi Collins**

Patterns

"Sell your cleverness and buy bewilderment."
-Rumi

The mind, the ego, the subconscious construct is often referred to as the great trickster. I want you to give yours a silly name. Something that doesn't have a lot of weight. So that every time you catch yourself being tricked, you can say, "oh not this time Simba. I'm in charge here." Remember, don't take anything seriously.

My ego's new name is: _____

The subconscious mind is a labyrinth of lies disguised as truths, of tainted memories weighted with emotion and a biased list of reactions waiting to immerge. It's full of some great programming as well. I describe it as a labyrinth because it isn't just one idea. But a series of twists and turns that protect your ego from being revealed. I have experience revealing this maze with the most narcissistic and the most selfless people. We all inadvertently create these mazes by protecting ourselves from embarrassment or disapproval, by avoiding something in our hearts or by losing ourselves in the opinions of others.

These negative and limiting programs are very sneaky. **Just because you can prove something or validate its existence, doesn't mean it serves your highest truth.** Be vigilant for the repeated patterns in your life. It is your mission to not be fooled by the trickster. Not to try to outsmart it, but simply to see where it is keeping you back from being the best you, then calmly correcting it.

Did you know that nearly 95% of your decisions are made subconsciously? What a wild notion to really ponder. Can you even fathom that? I remind myself regularly who is typically at the wheel, and it helps to thwart guilt. Understanding the maze of your subconscious is pertinent to your growth.

Curious as to how this maze became a program in the first place? What creates the patterns in your life? What tools are you currently using to shape your personality? When something bad happens, do you use guilt or shame to make sure it doesn't happen again? When you have something important to do, do you use procrastination or fear to sabotage yourself? Are these negative tools used as your motivators? Well, they are great for keeping you stuck in your loop.

Sit back and analyze your life. The "mistakes" you've made, the experiences you've missed out on, the things you're holding yourself back from. Look for those songs in your head you've played on repeat. The doubt and the negativity that you've repeated over the years.

Next, think about everything you've achieved. From school, to sports, to work, and everyday life choices. If you have kids, if you've had relationships, learned skills, how did you do it? Think about learning new skills especially because this is how you've managed to motivate yourself.

List some accomplishments below and think about the weeks/months/years leading up to those moments. How did you treat yourself? Were you kind? Were you excited or afraid?

_____

_____

_____

_____

_____

Do you motivate yourself with a carrot at the end of a stick, with your eyes on the prize? Or, are you like most people suffering, and are motivated by guilt or fear? Maybe you get too drunk, feel like garbage the next day, hate yourself for another day, then work like crazy to feel accomplished and productive for a few days, only to race towards the weekend to repeat the horrible process all over again.

Another common pattern I see is where one will feel terrible, take their fear, anger, frustration out on those closest to them. Then, of course they feel even worse because of their behavior, and then attempt to do everything they can to mend the wounds they've caused. Depleting their energy and self-worth by seeking the approval and admiration from others, leaving them feeling empty again. So, they repeat the pattern and the cycle continues.

Remember the orange story. What comes out of us was already inside. Are you addicted to feeling badly? Most people are.

Notice how the trend is horizontal, like a roller coaster, up and down without growth. Like a heart monitor during a panic attack, your life may feel like a series of random ups and downs. Maybe you've managed to add an incline in there, but if you're using these negative motivators, your line is trending more horizontal than it needs to be. The two pictures below show what life might be like for you right now, on a fixed path, and how life will be as you continue your journey through this program.

Breaking Patterns for Growth

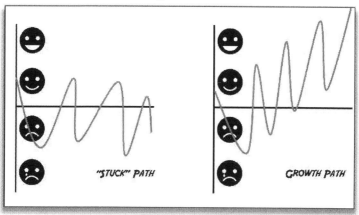

"STUCK" PATH

GROWTH PATH

Figure 2: Breaking Patterns for Growth: As you continue on the path of growth, life's downs don't seem to go as low or last as long, and the ups become more frequent and last longer. Whereas before the downs seemed to last longer and the ups would be gone far too quickly. Does this look familiar?

As an exercise, I want you to write down your limiting beliefs. Remember that you need to look at these things with less weight. These characteristics belong to "Simba", your ego. Limiting beliefs are any thoughts, facts or feelings that don't serve your growth. These are not who you really are any more and we are going to work these out of your system. So, write them down lightly and smile as you do.

_____

_____

_____

_____

_____

_____

_____

_____

_____

_____

> *"Khail was the missing piece to my puzzle! He provided much needed insight once I finally got the courage to take the leap into my health journey. If you're like I was and forever the pessimist, you must talk to Khail. I cannot recommend him highly enough and after suffering from crippling anxiety, panic attacks and agoraphobia for well over 20 years, I think I am a pretty good judge."*
> **-Fiona Grabowskyj**

Uncovering Your Negative Motivators

*"We cannot solve our problems with the same thinking
we used when we created them."*
-Albert Einstein

We need to dive deeply into your life to understand the specific patterns you utilize. To start, let's go over some of the most common patterns and motivators that I've helped people crush!

The most common and most destructive negative motivator is **Guilt**. Perhaps your mother would say, "oh don't worry, I will clean this up," or your father would say "oh no, let me take care of this, my bad back can handle it". Our parents, our teachers, our society, everywhere we look we see guilt being used as an incentive.

But guilt bears negativity. Guilt leaves you frozen in time, unable to get past the **regret** you've experienced. It causes you to go back again and again to the same problems you wish you could avoid. When we guilt someone else, we are trying to make them feel bad, to get them to do something good. Guilt is selfish in this way. When we guilt ourselves, we are holding back our potential, as negativity brings us down and robs us of so much.

The past can never be undone. No matter what you do, you couldn't have done it differently. You used the tools you had available at the given time. Even if you were absent minded, even if you froze and knew better, you used the toolset you had at the time. Perhaps your toolset was too full of doubt. Knowing this still leaves you with an awful feeling, right? This feeling is primal. It dates back to a time when mistakes could mean life or death, where problems had solutions, and when there wasn't an abundance of terrible options at your fingertips.

Even the very logic of guilt is absurd. You're supposed to feel bad for something you cannot change? To beat guilt, focus on what you will do next time. Do what you can and accept/allow the rest. Also, take pride in all your choices because if they hurt, they are excellent lessons to learn from. And you LOVE lessons, don't you? This bad feeling is there for your own good. Use your Pause Breaths to interrupt the pattern that guilt brings on. Visualize a successful next time. Love yourself by being at peace with your decisions and consistently remind yourself that you are growing!

The next is **worry.** We worry about our health, our finances, our children. We worry about our spouses. We worry what others think. Worst of all are the worriers that worry because there's nothing to worry about. This is one of the most addictive motivators. People think, "if I'm not worried about planning this, I will surely forget something." No, you will only add a layer of suffering that will blind you from the beautiful thing you're planning in the first place. I also hear, "but how will they know I care if I don't worry?" Remember the difference between caring and worrying. I see worry everywhere, with weddings, vacations, and especially worrying about those closest to you.

Worrying about others comes with a level of selfishness as well. It is closely tied to guilt and we often interlace the two. When you put your worries on others, you are taking from them. When you worry to yourself, you are wasting up all your productive time fearing something that hasn't even happened, and probably never will.

What could you be doing with all that time? Caring is productive and proactive. One of the biggest reasons I can help anyone no matter their schedule is because beating anxiety is about doing so much less! Less suffering, less fear, less wasted time on the unlikely or the inevitable.

> *"I'm an old man with many troubles, most of which have never happened."*
> - Mark Twain

Combating worrying is about controlling what you can and accepting what you can't. Embrace the realization that sometimes there is nothing you can do except control your state of being. Tell yourself "I refuse to waste my life, to give up my time, feeding into fear and needless, empty worrying."

When you are not accepting, you are resisting.

Ask yourself, "is resisting the unknown or resisting the inevitable, serving me? Does it make sense? Will it help me grow?"

One of the biggest things I see with people resisting is asking **why.** People ask, "why am I having these feelings?" or "why does my head go there when that happens?" or if only I knew *why* I had anxiety, but rarely are they trying to figure out **what** to do or **how** to get better. Asking why becomes an addiction as well. Rather than accepting and taking a step forward, asking why takes the sufferer down a rabbit hole of more questions. It's important to bring this up again because it is a repeat offender you will want to be vigilant for.

The truth is that no answer will make anything better. Expecting the right words to help is like expecting to get drenched from reading the word water. Action in the positive direction is the answer to this resistance. Putting the right foot forward to eliminate the debilitating pattern, rather than dwell on its existence, is your solution!

When you ask why, you are validating the existence of your fear. Do you really think it needs more validation? As you answer the question "why", you're empowering the fear, adding facts and memories only creates more weight.

The next time you find yourself asking why, switch gears and ask yourself "what" you could be doing to solve this problem. You might wake up tomorrow and feel terrible. You might stand up and feel dizzy. Maybe you're weeks into the process and still unable to accept that this is just how your body is right now, but you are working to change it, and all will be well soon. You must accept this. You must not pretend to be surprised when you fall back into old habits. You must stop asking why! Tell yourself, "I am working to get better!", and only ask "what can I do to get even better?"

There will always be ups and downs. Don't get lost in the downs because of an addiction to asking why.

You have a list of "why" questions floating in your head. Go ahead and write them below. Then, reframe your questions to be positive affirmations in the spaces below. These affirmations need to resonate with you and they need to be true. Write them with an intention to feel good when saying them. For example, change "why do I get anxious in the car?" to "I am a great driver and I love the freedom to go where I please whenever I wish!"

_____

_____

_____

_____

_____

_____

_____

_____

_____

_____

_____

_____

_____

The next pattern I see has to do with **pity and self-worth.** These are very sneaky, but this lesson was incredibly eye-opening for me and truly started me on the fast-track to self-improvement.

Have you ever NEEDED to get your point across? Do you ever feel like nobody understands you and you always have great ideas? Perhaps you didn't get enough attention as a child or this is your current experience at work with a boss or at home with your family?

This is self-pity. When we suffer over not being heard, not being cared about, not being seen, we are telling ourselves that we are worth so much more than what we are experiencing. This over-exaggerated sense of self-worth backfires and makes us feel terrible. We pity ourselves, feeling sorry for how small we feel. But you are not small or weak. You may feel depleted or empty, but these aren't true either. Your habits and perspectives are just off a little. You may think that this isn't you. Don't let your gut tell you that you don't pity yourself if you clearly suffer from the struggles that lead to it.

To combat this, be respectful of different opinions. Cherish the beauty that is contrast around you. Be grateful that everyone isn't you, for how lame life would be if this were so. Be confident in your decisions by welcoming the different opinions and reflecting on the truth that others see. Don't feel sorry for yourself when you are not heard. You are heard. You can hear yourself. Your worth comes from within you, not from what others think. Think about your need to be heard as a need for validation, whether it's your intelligence, sense of humor or value you, it is all misdirected. Swallow your explanations. Pause Breath interrupt that pattern. Be proud of your individuality. **Notice as that need fades that you were putting your worth into the hands of others.**

The limiting factor here is NEED. Don't need anything except the necessities. We need air, food and water. Confusing a want with a need is where the tension comes from. Your self-worth will grow when you prove to yourself that your thoughts are great, and you don't need validation from others. Your self-love will increase by not seeking outside approval or recognition. This is you filling the void all by yourself. Your Pause Breaths and positive thought insertion for breaking these patterns can be used to feed into your growth. More will be explained soon.

Victimhood takes us back to responsibility. You are not a victim. You are powerful. You carry the power to experience the way you choose to experience. If you're in pain, tired, late, angry, or anything you deem as negative and you believe it is because of something outside of your control, or someone else is to blame, you are victimizing yourself, telling your subconscious mind that you are small or incapable, and you're limiting your potential. You are the gatekeeper of your experience. If somebody rear-ends you, sure, you couldn't do anything about that, but you can choose to suffer about it using anger against the other driver or fear to block you from driving again. Or you can choose to be proactive, to live in peace, to feed the good wolf, and to grow!

Being a victim makes you think of yourself as incapable. It makes you believe you are stuck, that your mind is fixed, and you are limited. It makes you lazy. If you feel like you need someone, you need support, or you need something from the outside world, you will always be victimizing yourself. **Understand that you are all that you need and that you are the best support you could ever ask for.** Ever notice how you are always there when you need you the most? When you are alone and lost, there's that little spark that hasn't given up yet. That is the true you. Unbreakable. Your friends and family play a wonderful role and it is great to have someone to talk to, but trust me when I tell you that you are more powerful than the ears or crying shoulders of others can ever be.

Self-sabotage comes in many forms. It is important to develop a desire to push yourself in the right direction, to create leverage in your life with pleasure rather than pain. There's the difference between motivation and inspiration. When you're inspired, you are being curiously, lovingly or extatically pulled toward your goal. But when we are motivated, we are pushed to do something, hustling, or driving. If we are using any of these negative drivers as motivators, we will always be limiting our potential. Lead yourself to success with positivity.

"With joy you will draw water from the wells of salvation."
-Isaiah 12:3

This simply means that we need to approach our goals with love, happiness, and peace if we want to enjoy and fulfill them. Your salvation is in the act of joy, in the very practice of it, rather than in an experience in which you use to allow yourself to feel joyful. You are the creator of your experience. Joy comes from inside of you, just like the orange analogy. This is one of those sections you will want to reread. I have a way of making the complex sound simple. Don't glaze over a lesson that could change your life! I will elaborate on a few of these as well.

Fear

"If I have lost confidence in myself, I have the universe against me."
-Ralph Waldo Emerson

Fear can play a major role in our decision making. But fear is an interesting concept. It is said that fear is no different than excitement to the body, but **the mind determines whether something is good or bad**. You can see how responsibility comes into the picture again here! Same chemicals, same processes, but perspective will decide the translation of the experience.

"Man's immortality is not to live forever; for that wish is born of fear. Each moment free from fear makes a man immortal."
-Alexander the Great

How is fear holding you back? How has it kept you from growing? Can you feel how freeing life would be without fear? Just think of a time you were lost in fun. Roller coaster? A hard belly laugh? Don't you dare let your mind trick you into feeling sorry for yourself when I ask about this stuff! You just admit that when you're without fear, you're free, and we will help get you there. I love you. Sorry for yelling.

Remember that fear is contagious and that it is a primal instinct to share fear. It is almost as if people love to connect with others who share the same fears. Slapping five over hating snakes or fearing panic attacks. A funny thing people say is, "oh no, I hate my fears, you don't understand how much I hate panic attacks." What kind of weight do you think this silly sentence holds? It's heavy! And useless! I say silly because of course you hate that. Remember, hate is your prison. That compulsion to voice your hate is an affirmation, and remember that to the mind, you are saying that this fear is important to you, and you would love to experience more related to it.

Feeding into fear becomes very addicting. The mind creates programs and patterns to perpetuate the horrible what-ifs, and thus the fear is affirmed again and again. But our understanding of the way the brain works, this only absorbing, always optimizing machine tells us that this is all making things worse. How many times do you think you really need to analyze the fear you have? If you're afraid of public speaking, how's rehearsing the FEELING of fear affecting you? How does ruminating on your fears serve you? What is it doing to your state of being, your relationships, and everything else?

Fear is essentially useless. Respect, on the other hand, is useful. You can respect the things that can hurt you by not taking them for granted. I respect the tiger enough not to tease it. But fear takes hold of you, cripples you, constricts you and limits you.

People often fear loss. They fear gain and success as well. Essentially, people fear change. Because any change is translated as potentially life-threatening to the brain.

A body in fear is a body hunched over, with chin tucked and shoulders forward. Fear is quiet, shallow breathing. Does this sound like someone you used to know? This posture encourages fear in the body. But by now, doing your routine pause-breaths with your chin up, shoulders back and spine erected, you may realize how often your posture and breathing are representing a state of peace! Keep practicing!

People suffer from "what if's", but "if" means Imaginary Fear. We are inviting in suffering here. If the bad thing actually does happen, now you've suffered twice. For instance, if you're afraid you may lose your elderly grandma, and for weeks you mope around in pain, fearing the worst, creating PTSD for every single chyme your phone makes assuming to hear "that call", you're creating a ton of completely useless suffering. You will even treat grandma quite differently through fear, being timid, fragile, and distant due to thinking about the inevitable. It may even put you into a selfish state around her, needing her reassurance. All the time leading up to that moment is spent in negativity. Then she passes, and you realize you've spent months in agony, and now you're going to repeat it. Worst of all, those months could have been spent in love, making the very best out of the situation. Living for grandma, encouraging her, helping her last days be some of her best. The what ifs, fears and worries are robbing you and those around you! When you feel yourself stuck in a loop, Pause Breath that pattern and focus on the good. Visualize the experience you wish to have You can do this! Practice.

In the next few sections, you will be tapping into some more practical applications you can start applying to your mind so that you can begin to rewire your entire experience! These practices are towards the end of this program because it isn't easy to apply them without establishing the foundational techniques explained in the beginning. It all has purpose.

Death is that one thing that we all have in common, yet nobody wants to talk about. We create a society around extending life, without actually living life, and ignoring that one inevitable experience. For something so common, you would think that we would celebrate it. It is the moment that we know we no longer have pain or suffering. We become completely free from all negativity, all traumatic memories, all responsibilities. Regardless of your beliefs, it could easily be looked at as a good thing.

Some live 80 years. Others live the same day, for 80 years.

Look at death as a definite. Know you will die. And use this very basic knowledge to remind yourself to live while you are alive. Sit with it and be real. It takes some getting used to, but it will be liberating.

When someone dies, understand the basic principal that they will never suffer again. Use your understanding of reality to remember them for all the good that you shared with them, so that your memories are warm and inviting. Remember them the way they would want you to, or better, the way you honestly want to. Feed the good wolf. You are the gatekeeper to your experience. In the years to follow, you will be happy you focused so hard on love rather than pain as the positive memories randomly pop into your head, fueling tears of joy.

When your thoughts go toward planting negative memories, Pause Breath that pattern and plant the seeds you wish to grow.

If you fear the death of someone, it's the same reminder. Why not live every moment to the fullest with this person? Remember what worry does. Why waste your time in dread?

If something is inevitable, why live in fear? Learn to accept it. Learn to live with it. And learn to actually live while knowing this thing is coming. How? Pause Breaths and practice focusing on the higher-truth over and over until you're satisfied with reality. Don't be a victim to your old wiring. We only have one shot at this life as far as we know. Why not make the best of it for you and those around you?

Know this: you are strong, you are capable, and you are limitless. Take time to be real with yourself. You may find much of your anxiety is released when you get real about death. Remember, you can't fool the subconscious. Your feelings are telling.

Take some time to identify some of your major fears and self-sabotaging behaviors. Reflect. How do these serve you? What are you going to do differently?

My Fears Reframed

Bonus #4: FEEL It (Health Anxiety)

Look at you go, unlocking all my precious "secrets". Okay so you've read about death. That IS where your health anxiety is coming from. I wanted to add another section to this bonus. It is called **"Are You Begging to be Labeled?"** Our society, the media and the construc5t of the ego have brainwashed us into thirsting for a diagnosis. A common phenomenon occurs when one has seen the 13th cardiologist and the diagnosis always comes back clear. People become disappointed! Careful what you wish for.

As you notice your physical symptoms that you don't like, after making sure you are in fact heathy, Pause Breath, put your hand over your heart, and tell yourself that you love yourself. Tell yourself "I am healthy, I love you Khail Kapp (feel free to swap my name for yours), I love my life, all is well." When you pass a mirror, look deeply into your eyes and utilize the same practice. Remember, go slow and **feel it.**

Look, there's a reason why happier cancer patients are more likely to survive. If your body sees that you enjoy living, it will reciprocate. You have so much power. Lead yourself with love! Do this daily, use facts that back it up, and go easy on yourself. Remember, don't take life so seriously.

Defining Your Ideal Self

"Change your conception of yourself and you will automatically change the world in which you live."
-Neville Goddard

As you take time to identify all the patterns, the limiting beliefs and fears in your life, remember not to become discouraged. Through keeping up with the foundation, mindfulness will continue to reveal these patterns to you. You will notice them more and more. It isn't that you are worse than you thought. This is simply your conscious awareness expanding. Congratulations!

We need to be able to see the leaks in the ship if we are to sail to new lands.

As you notice the negative be mindful of the positive in your life. What do you like about yourself? What would you love to see more of? Do you want to be more outgoing? Honest? Loving? Do you want to be more grateful?

Your desires for what you do want will be your compass and the winds in your sails.

I've attached an image below you can use to better represent who you really are, and what's standing in the way of being this version of you full-time. Take a moment to list some personality traits that no longer serve you, and some experiences that may have conditioned those traits on Figure 3.

More importantly, you want to describe your ideal self. Do this after reading the entire section (see space provided after Figure 3). Your ideal self is the self without mental illness, without the short fuse, jealousy or judgment. The person you wish to be today or the person you are happy to grow towards. Perhaps it is the person you always wanted to be or believed you were as a child. In the next section, we will begin to rewire your mind to be this person!

To get started on this practice now, **replace your positive thought insertion** (after every timed Pause Breath and during your morning and evening routines) **with a vision of your ideal self**. If you've practiced Pause Breaths regularly for a week or so, and you've developed that ability to feel calm and good simply by breathing, this should be a fairly easy transition. To test yourself, what's changed? Have you been able to bow out of an argument that you never would have? Have you scrolled past some fear that normally would have taken up an afternoon of research? The transition from visualizing something easily positive to something you wish to come true is much easier when you've practiced. If you find it difficult to feel good about your ideal self, stick with the box of kittens for now.

Your ideal self should be very detailed. Starting internal, what are your character traits and abilities? What is your mood? What is your energy level like? How's your health and what does your body feel like? What are you wearing? What are you doing? What does the environment sound like and smell like?

Know that the most powerful statement in the human language is "I Am". Affirming what you are on a regular basis can build you up, or it can crush you. Whoever you want to be, whether it is brave, patient, happy, you must affirm this regularly by telling yourself "I am strong" or "I am worthy." At the same time, stop telling yourself you are who you do not want to be. Quit saying "I suck", "I am scared", "I can't", and "I can't even".

You can even.

There's a fine line between honesty and self-deprecation. Rather than try to differentiate which one you are being, stop affirming you are anything that you do not want to be. These concepts are difficult to retain. Please read these sections thoroughly as they will change your life forever!

The Real You

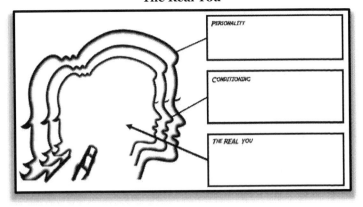

Figure 3: The Real You. Your personality is a mask. Your ego is a combination of this and your conditioning. But the real you, your ideal self, the you you're aspiring to become fully remains untouched beneath the unnecessary.

Use this section to define your ideal self!

_____
_____
_____
_____
_____
_____
_____
_____
_____
_____
_____
_____
_____
_____
_____
_____
_____
_____

> *"After silently following Khail for months, I was struck by anxiety at a funeral. I decided that now was as good a time as ever. I reached out to him and he helped me find the courage to leave the car, attend the funeral, and call him back. After some coaching calls and working through his course, my years of phobias in restaurants and public places are gone! I've grown so much in just a few months. Thank you, brother!"*
> **-Fabian Sanchez**

Practical Negativity Eliminators

Those that were dancing appeared insane
to those that couldn't hear the music.

By mastering mindfulness through the Pause Breath, you are now ready to use this set of skills to get past, eliminate or capitalize on all the negativity in your life. Some people will think this is going too far. They'll say "Khail, the world isn't all rainbows and kittens." But this is only partly true. The world is full of rainbows and kittens! And it doesn't matter what the world is full of. Your state of being depends on what YOU are full of. Now that you know how the subconscious mind works, know that the mind only works with the materials it has.

On a dreary morning, a drunken ronin walked aimlessly along an empty road when a monk appeared. The ronin, being very depressed, stopped the monk and begged for guidance. He asked, "Is there such thing as heaven? If yes, is there such thing as hell and am I doomed to go there?"

The monk retorted, "Who are you but a drunken brute? You couldn't even begin to understand such insightful things. Be gone from my presence and don't waste my time!"

Enraged, the ronin drew his sword. As he prepared for a kill, the monk calmly said, "this is hell."

Taken back, the ronin's face softened. He sheathed his sword, calmed his gaze and humbly bowed before the monk. The monk smiled, touched the ronin on the shoulder and said, "this, is heaven."

If you want to live in a peaceful world, you will need to start seeking peace, and seeing it in every experience. You must **be peace.** As you practice, it becomes easier, more natural, and fun.

You may not be able to *brainwash* yourself into believing the world is 100% good. But you can certainly rewire your mind to see MUCH more of it.

If there were a 'Surgeon General's Warning' on every bad news story, every sad song and every person that is still addicted to negativity, this might be easier. But for those situations that take a little bit of tact, I am going to share with you a few amazing techniques.

The first is to completely remove the negativity. If you are about to engage in an argument, interrupt that pattern with a Pause Breath, excuse yourself or bow out. If you feel the NEED to validate, remember to ask yourself whether you want to be right or happy. If you can press pause and ask everyone to join you in calming down and breathing, if you can walk away, change the subject, or simply tune it out, do it. Use your children! They love the Pause Breath!

For the times that it is you against your thoughts, you must affirm that these are yours and not you. You are the observer of these thoughts. Label the thoughts and feelings as they come to you. Both good and bad. Practice saying, "I am experiencing some negative thought right now." Don't get caught up in it. Sit back and watch it. **Narration** like this can pull you out of a subconscious loop and remove that heavy emotional weight. This is a fantastic practice in mindfulness.

Before practiced mindfulness, we are slaves to the limbic system.

By not getting caught up in a negative thought, and the heavy feeling, you weaken it. **Thoughts derive their power from the attention we give them.** When you say, "I hate feeling this way", remember that you are asking for more, you are giving power to that feeling, and you are telling your subconscious that "this is important to me". Don't beat yourself up over random thoughts either. **Always be kind to yourself** and you will make this intrusive thinking weaker and eventually nonexistent.

If the feelings and thoughts seem overwhelming, one of my favorite tactics is to meet it with even <u>more energy</u>. So much energy that it becomes ridiculous. See if you can make yourself laugh by **over-exaggerating** your fear to a ludicrous level. For instance, if you are afraid of getting dizzy, tell yourself that you will get so dizzy that you will vomit everywhere. That everyone will see this and vomit as well. Cut to the next scene and the news reporters are covering a dizzy vomiting epidemic that is spreading all over the world. People are slipping out of grocery stores and shopping centers. Maybe a little gross, but it takes your mind off the negative and takes your gut out of the control that the feeling may have over you. This should all be done mentally while Pause Breathing throughout. Talking rapidly out loud will only instigate the anxiety. Keep in mind that you want to slow the body down.

If you're afraid of driving, imagine that you forget to check your speed and the next thing you know, 12 police cars are chasing you. You realize that you are too far in to stop now. Your phone rings and someone with a masked voice is giving you instructions on where to stash the diamonds that you now realize are in your backseat.

If your self-talk is scary, give it a **comical voice**. Remember that you should have a silly name for your ego? Pretend that Marvin the Martian is now telling you that you are not good enough, or that anxiety has power over you. Are you really going to listen to that little guy? <u>This method is incredibly powerful and should not be overlooked!</u>

By diverting your attention and getting lost in a story, you grip on your fears, worries and anxieties will loosen. This same mindset can be used in the opposite direction, giving your fear a ridiculously positive spin. If you fear going outside, imagine that when you leave the house, the world is going to be there clapping for you. They put a medal around your neck and crown you queen of the universe with an unlimited supply of Doritos. The key here is that you are taking the wheel of your conscious awareness. Don't divert your attention with your phone or anything else outside of you.

Whatever you decide to do the next time negative thoughts and fears pop into your head, make sure that you don't take it too seriously. Self-love means treating yourself kindly, so you must meet the negative with love. If someone is opposing your opinions or criticizing your work, rather than getting caught up in your head, focus on them and the message and meet it with love. Immediately be appreciative that they would take precious time out of their day to help you. Forget their intentions. Forget the history or hierarchy with this person. Pay attention to loving the ability to experience this. Walk away and fill your thoughts with gratitude and think well of them. Then, from a good place, check to see if you can learn anything from their criticism. Be proud that you separated your new and ideal self from a more sensitive and fearful version.

Remember, the mind works with the tools it has. Love them. Love the contrast. And above everything, love yourself. Feed your mind love and positivity and you will not only feel better, you will experience this love more and more.

For the negative that is out of your control, like the horrific news stories or someone's sad post on social media (things you might want to consider unfollowing), understand this very basic, but very challenging concept: **No number of tears shed can make someone feel happier.** No amount of sorrow can undo what has been done. As a primal society, it was pertinent for our survival to share life-threatening information. But now, people believe that sharing the knowledge of a school bus accident, or a tornado that destroyed a town hundreds of miles away, that this knowledge is somehow powerful. But until you learn not to feel it, and to only react to it if you can help in some way, you may want to avoid it.

By crying for others, by maximizing your empathy towards the problems you cannot change, you are only wiring your mind to experience more of that. More feelings of incapability, more beliefs that the world is full of misery and despair. The further you travel along this journey of strength and positivity, you may realize just how much of the world thrives off pain and suffering. Do not feel alone. Be the light unto the darkness.

"Be the change you wish to see in the world."
-Mahatma Gandhi

This is the best you can do. And you may be surprised sometimes at just how much deep down your friends and family truly want to experience happiness when they are wallowing in useless suffering. Attempting to focus on the good may be the breath of fresh air they were looking for. But don't spend your energy trying to change them.

Focus on your energy, and watch as your presence becomes the gift they didn't know they needed.

> "Khail is seriously AMAZING! I've had anxiety and agoraphobia for the last 15 years or so! Knowing he has been through a similar ordeal makes him very easy to talk to. He is always positive and extremely supportive! I am now able to leave my house, drive and do things I never thought I would be able to do again! I can finally LIVE again! He is a true inspiration and the real deal!!! THANK YOU, Khail for all you do!"
> **-Lara Easterling**

Discovering the Higher-Self and Purpose

"I saw the angel in the marble and carved until I set him free. Every block of stone has a statue inside and it is the task of the sculptor to discover it."
-Michelangelo (on carving David)

Remember the imagery in Figure 3, where the real you remains untouched? Michelangelo meant that to find the beauty within anything, one must shed the useless. Shed whatever doesn't serve you.

Many who suffer from mental illness are at war with themselves. They have problems that (they don't even realize) are very much in their power to solve. In fact, I'd argue that every problem you face is within your power to solve. The catch is our definition of what a problem is. I see them as opportunities. I must. I can't imagine wasting a moment in pity when I could be taking steps towards growth. Problems are giant stepping stones. And I know what you're thinking, "here's another coach/guru/handsome/cunning... (wait maybe that's what I'm thinking...) here's another guy telling me problems are opportunities, but he has no idea what it is like for me!" But I do. I've helped people out of the craziest situations. The stories I've heard, even my own personal path, it is all riddled with opportunities. Do I capitalize immediately every single time? Heck no. **We all fall off the horse. But we can either roll around in the mud, or we can get back on.** Eventually, you must move forward. Sooner or later that problem becomes your catalyst for change. Might as well decide to react to it appropriately immediately and save yourself the heartache.

Inside of your mind, there is a scale. We tilt the scales negatively and positively with every experience. Continually outweighing the negative with positive will ultimately lead to a happier, healthier mind. A mind that begins to look for the good and experience more pleasure. A body that delivers an abundance of energy and security. A behavior that embodies confidence and love. All of these will be created from within. Your beliefs are your reality.

"When I let go of who I am, I become who I might be."
-Lao Tzu

By shedding the negative, by removing the labels that do not serve you, and by finding exactly what does, you will start to become something so much more than you can currently imagine. It's true. Our consciousness can't comprehend a greater consciousness through the lens of a lesser consciousness. We cannot fathom being more aware than we are now.

Take my word for it. The work you're putting into yourself right now will be more rewarding than you can imagine.

There's something curious that more than half of my clients share. They're often awakened at the same time every single night. Typically, between 2-4:30am, they wake up for no apparent reason, and then have a hard time falling back to sleep. Whatever your religious or spiritual beliefs, I think we can all agree that during that time of night, the chatter of the mind is most silent. Whether it is your higher-self, God, ghosts, a noisy cat outside, or anything, there is an opportunity to learn about yourself by waking up from a deep sleep. Where do you think your thoughts come from?

"The breezes at dawn have secrets to tell you. Do not go back to sleep.
You must ask for what you really want. Do not go back to sleep."
-Rumi

What you might think of as a weird habit, I believe it is your calm subconscious mind telling you that you to follow your purpose. Not necessarily something predestined, but perhaps something that you developed as a child. Your purpose may simply be the output of your brain after years of input. It often feels like a burning desire for something more, being a part of something greater than yourself and that maybe there is more that you can be doing.

As a practice, the next few times you are awakened like this, get out of bed. Do something inspirational like draw, color, go for a walk, meditate, pray, breathe, dance, or whatever you can do to make your heart sing. Journaling may be the best option as writing whatever comes to your mind may be exactly what the subconscious wants to reveal to you. For now, see this as an **opportunity** to plant a few more positive seeds in your mind. Do a few Pause Breaths to get back to sleep. In time, I truly believe that you will discover yourself thriving more in life or being pulled towards something greater if you follow my instructions in this book, and learn to follow your heart. I've seen it time and time again.

> *"You don't cross paths with people by accident! I'm forever*
> *grateful to connect with Khail. His coaching, inspiration*
> *and support have been so helpful. His course is the most*
> *AMAZING thing I have ever done for myself. I learned so*
> *much about myself and continue to put everything into*
> *practice. I am feeling better than I have in YEARS!!!"*
> **-Courtney Strong**

Rewiring the Subconscious Mind

"You need to hear this loud and clear: No one is coming. It is up to you."
-Mel Robbins

Now that you're ready for change, it is time to tell you how to do it! But secretly, if you've been doing everything that I've instructed so far, if you've been keeping up with morning and evening routines, performing Pause Breaths 10 or more times daily, drinking enough water, keeping up with the Brag Book, and practicing all the assignments, you have been rewiring your mind this whole time! Usually I recommend this section between 2-4 weeks after beginning the foundation, but it is perfectly fine for you to pick these lessons up and apply them to your life anytime. It just may be an even steeper climb to try to take these on without the foundational practices.

If you haven't started with the foundation yet, take a moment to practice some Pause Breaths. There are no mistakes. Better late than never. Set that alarm and do the foundational practices mentioned in the beginning. Also, keep up with that Brag Book! I apologize for the redundancy but I REALLY WANT YOU WELL!!! So, if I have to remind you at this book's expense, it's worth it.

You may now have a beautiful understanding of what reality is and how life works for you. Mindfulness, experience as a choice and responsibility alone can turn your entire life around. To implement the practices, you have been using the Pause Breath as a pattern interrupt and starting ritual. Each time you run into a negative situation, a pattern you no longer wish to experience, a feeling that might be holding you back, interrupt with a mindful breath. Follow it with visualization of a preferred outcome or simply something that makes you happy.

Consistent visualization and affirmation of the person you want to be, the way you wish to see or experience the world, or simply a practiced positive feeling, will rewire your mind to experience more of that. To change your beliefs, you must start with the right thoughts. Putting enough thought into something will elicit the appropriate feeling. As mentioned earlier, feelings are chemicals and will soon change the wiring in your nervous system.

Your beliefs will become reality with consistency.

As a practice, use the imagery attached to this section. In Figure 4A, define as many positive thoughts as you can that elicit the right feelings and change your beliefs. Figure 4B maps the process needed to create the logical mindset you wish to have. An example of something **logical** would be "just relax". It's logical, but it may feel impossible at times. The **results** would be the behavior you want to display and what it will mean for your life. Perhaps improved relationships, promotions or healthier physique. The **actions** you take towards achieving those results are fairly self-explanatory. What would the anxiety-free version of yourself do to arrive at a destination comfortably? Practicing on different roads and conditions. Volunteering to drive the family cross country. Continue to work backwards mapping these two figures out.

As another example, let's say you want to be calmer in public. Your **results** would be feeling really good and relaxed in conversations. Your **actions** would be having meaningful, relaxed, and engaged conversation with others. Your **beliefs** would be "**I am** calm, confident, interesting, present and engaged". Write each of these individually for emphasis. Your **feelings** would be similar, all positive, and would be framed as "I feel calm and I feel confident". Describe what those feelings will do for you and how they feel. Describe how they will affect others! The **thoughts** will always have the most content because this is the ammunition we create. Thoughts are what we can control. For both images, you want to maximize the thought process in the positive direction.

Rewiring the Subconscious

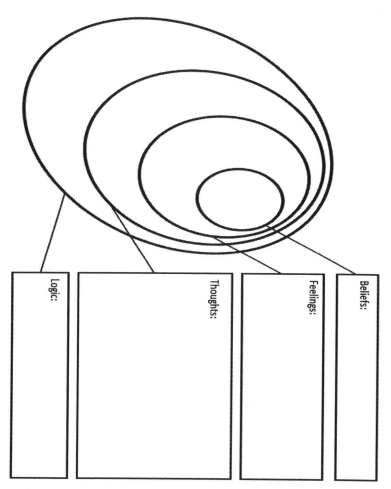

Figure 4A: Rewiring the Subconscious. This demonstrates beliefs being the core of who we are. Then each layer outward is more superficial in meaning, and more easily manipulated.

Rewiring the Subconscious Continued

Figure 4B: Rewiring the Subconscious Continued. This is an amazing brain rewiring tool, brought to you in the form of a plotted line graph that is shaped like a man looking down at his phone. Take this idea with you to help you break down a "problem" and work your mind towards an opportunity!

Take your bullet points from Figure 4B and write them out like a short story or paragraph you can ponder. For **social anxiety**, it should sound something like "I love engaging in meaningful conversation because it makes life worth living. My friends and family appreciate my contribution and I appreciate theirs. There is never a dull moment, even in the silence. I work to appreciate and enjoy the present moments I share with them. I seek to understand their contributions by asking plenty of insightful questions. I feel excited, energized and free when I reflect on this version of myself I've created, and I can tell that others enjoy this me as well. My thoughts always lean towards being a brighter light in the room." And the list can go on. This is easiest to fill out as the negative and limiting beliefs pop into your head. Interrupt those patterns with your Pause Breath, and starting with knowing what you do want, work your way down and fill your mind with the right thoughts. This can also work in reverse depending on how the ideas flow to you. The method is more about learning to reframe your experience, learning how to create the higher-truth feelings, and having something concrete to keep you consistent.

Keep reframing your limiting beliefs until you realize that you are truly limitless.

Note: in figure 4B, the logic is always the advice that someone who never suffers from anxiety would give you. Like "just relax" or "you're fine". You will feel this logic sooner or later. Keep it simple. Be kind to yourself

Use these systems to create a new morning and evening routine for yourself. Practice Pause Breathing while rehearsing these thought tracks daily. Plant the seeds and remember that you must be patient with your crops. Respect and cherish the journey.

Remember to reframe everything for seeking pleasure rather than avoiding pain. If you are trying to lose weight, you don't say "I am cutting this out of my diet". You want to say, "I am working towards a beach body."

If you haven't already started to crush your triggers, now is the time to wire your mind to be trigger-less! **See, you are not a gun to be fired by some external source. You are the hand that pulls the trigger.** And when you fire your weapon, love, calm and confidence emerges.

Begin to consistently reframe every negative thought, limiting belief, fear and trigger for the positive. By pausing, breathing and reframing, your state of awareness and mindfulness will evolve to something greater. Look at all the control you will be creating in your life!

Rewiring for Confidence

"To acquire true self power, you have to feel beneath no one, be immune to criticism and be fearless."
-Deepak Chopra

You do not need to be the loudest person in the room to demonstrate confidence. In fact, you can be an incredibly confident introvert. Being quiet doesn't equate to meekness. Confidence is something you carry inside of you. It is a state of being. It is trust in yourself. It is self-love. It grows from knowing that there aren't problems but opportunities. It is a state-of-being rather than a state-of-thinking. The principals you've learned in this book are setting you up for a major confidence boost, but I'd like to give you some more self-loving practices!

Each time you wash your hands, look into the mirror, deeply into your eyes. Try to smile without using your mouth. Imagine you are wearing a mask and allow your eyes to glow a smile. Start with a smile if this is too tricky for you. Then, carry this feeling with you after you walk away. Continue to master it by lovingly and happily looking into your own eyes. As a practice, notice how contagious and welcoming this look is with others.

The true problem with any suffering is a lack in self-love.

Remember the lessons on equality with others, valuing the contrast, and not *needing* to be heard. Step back and assist others in shining. Ask questions that you genuinely would like to know the answers to. Ask yourself, "how can I open up the floor to let others flourish?" and watch as they do the same for you.

There's a very good chance that you've never spent this much time or commitment on yourself, or it has been far too long. Your confidence is rising. If you want to improve it even further, other than keeping up with your current work, try augmenting each of your pause breaths to affirm what you want specifically: "I am interesting", "I am attractive", "I am deserving or worthy". These last two are very common and liberating. Many people believe that they are unworthy, less than, or even cursed. Remember, you are what you believe.

Let's do an example. Perhaps you don't feel interesting. Saying, "I am interesting", will elicit a negative feeling because that ego is saying "not true!" But it is true. And we need to bridge that gap. Going back to figures 4A and 4B, what kind of thoughts could you think that would lead you to the right belief? Thoughts like, "I have opinions and when I share them, people are interested", "I have a unique perspective people might want to hear", and "people are interested in hearing what I have to say".

Presence

Befriend the now, the only true time you have ever known.

To know something is to understand it wholly, to see it clearly having walked through the entire experience. I recently climbed a mountain in Colorado where I discovered an amazing lesson (and had the most insane spiritually enlightening experience of my life). One doesn't know the mountain until they've climbed to the top and lived to talk about it. While I was climbing, I repeatedly guessed that it would only take me another hour or so to finish the climb. But as I continued, the terrain got trickier, the incline steepened, and my energy depleted. 6 hours after my first assumption of only needing another hour to finish this task, and I was pressed against the top of the mountain, laughing and crying.

The climb was incredibly dangerous, requiring every bit of my attention. After hours of being forced into the present, I had clarity and silence unlike anything I'd ever experienced. My mind was open, and I received wisdom in the form of lessons and inner-dialog for hours after the experience.

The present moment is the only true moment. We often live in other moments, and although they feel real to us, they aren't reliable and definitely aren't truth. The past is gone, but our attention to it makes it real. The future is impossible to know for sure, yet our worries often guide us towards the very future we are fearing.

The past is but a memory. The future is a fantasy. All that exists is the ever-unfolding present.

Take mindfulness a step further by working towards consistent awareness with clarity, calmness and inner-peace. High hills to climb but worth every step! **You must live in the present moment more and more to continue your climb.** Tip the scales to the present moment by noticing just how often you are lost in thought, whether it is day dreaming, exposing yourself completely to some form of media, reminiscing the past or contemplating the future. Then, with that awareness, pause and breathe and just be. Try to appreciate the world around you from a different perspective. Allow the world to move around you without labeling the things that you see or assuming you know every outcome. Simply being and breathing are amazing exercises to become more present, and less anxious.

There is no anxiety in presence.

Where in your life do you have plenty of time to practice being more present? Where can you get lost in an experience or stop to smell the roses? Answer: everywhere! Start with the dishes. Focus your attention on the task at hand while performing pause breaths. Slow the process down and appreciate the moment. When you brush your teeth, try to be very efficient. Feel the brush along your jaw. See the work you are doing in your mind. The next time you are eating, chew your food up to 30 times. Technically, this is recommended! If I am not being mindful, I am not even sure that I chew most food at all. Chewing your food more will bring you into the present, but it will also improve your gut health, giving you a direct positive effect towards beating anxiety. Washing dishes is also a great time to practice your Pause Breathing and being present with the task at hand and is my personal favorite time to practice. Why? Because dish washing, like many chores, feels like something I just need to get done with and move on. That is a nasty feeling to carry that bleeds into every aspect of our lives. Lose the idea that you *just need to get this done*. Start with the dishes.

Multi-tasking is only a skill if you can stop.

Try to notice something new every day. If you are in a cubical at work, find something small around you that you never really looked at. Practice the Pause Breath while scanning your environment.

Another great tip for learning more presence starts with narrating what you do and what you imagine. Say, "I am feeling the ground beneath my feet, bending my knees, twisting my hips. I am calmly and happily entering this room." This narration pulls you out of experiencing through subconscious, being a victim to your thoughts, and puts you into the driver's seat of being conscious awareness.

Take a step back from your thoughts when you are trying to be present with others. Admiring the loves of your life or the environment you are in, as if it were the first time seeing them, can bring you overwhelming waves of joy. When you put a piece of food in your mouth, pretend to be a food critic and try to really taste it for everything it is. When you shower, feel the individual streams of water bouncing off your skin. Are you getting this?

Make a conscious effort to do something in the present moment every single day.

Begin to use the present moment to eliminate your "triggers" and achieve your happiness goals. If driving is your fear, get out of your head by feeling the steering wheel and telling yourself a story on what you are experiencing. Consciously Pause Breathing throughout the experience, feeling the wheel, the seat, the belt, seeing and appreciating your surroundings, and by keeping the car quiet. Hear the engine and feel the vibration. *Feel it, feel it.* Smile and keep a confident posture.

We often overlook the abundance of data and details around us. We get lost in thought, in haste or anxiety and miss the overwhelming beauty and magic of life. **Tension blocks you from being.** But by seeking this beauty around, you'll loosen your grip on anxiety.

> *"Words can't express how grateful I am to Khail for helping me regain my sanity! His breathing exercises, video calls and content helped me so much. I never felt judged for how I felt. He simply helped me snap right into reality. Despite grieving, he helped me realize the great life I have and I even feel excited! I've learned to teach my mind not to overthink. Khail is the best!"*
> **-Jodi Lestat**

Need versus Want

"He knows peace who has forgotten desire."
-Bhagavad Gita

Most anxiety comes from feeling powerless, lacking control, or having a tight grip on expectations. The lesson of need versus want takes us back to the monkey story, where the monkey believed it NEEDED the fruit and couldn't let it go. In reality, it could've easily found something else to eat. Up until now, the monkey mind may have prevented you from your ability to differentiate need and want, and it may not have had the abilities to take on a **monk mindset.**

True control comes from changing the monkey mind to the monk mind.

When we mix up the definitions of need and want, we set ourselves up for negative feelings. We lose control. We get annoyed or discouraged. We get angry. To better understand how this might be playing a major role in your life, I'm going to share an example. When you get into the car, do you need the radio on? Do you need stimulation? Or do you just *like* listening to music? Don't answer this! Everyone says they just like listening to music. **To learn to be completely honest with yourself, test yourself, everywhere, always, and all ways.** Turn off the radio for your next drive and see what happens. Can you sit still comfortably, or do you NEED to sing or tap the wheel? Do you need to always be doing something? Or do you simply enjoy doing things? Chores, talking, sitting in a waiting room, using the bathroom. What do you need and what do you want in your life? Test yourself!

I was a chronic information absorber. Podcasts, YouTube videos, audio books... There's nothing wrong with thirsting for knowledge if you merely want to become more intelligent. But if you can't just do the dishes in silence, if you're unable to walk outside without grabbing your phone or day dreaming something productive, you lack power and control, and ultimately your need to be distracted is fueling anxiety. To combat this, interrupt these patterns with your Pause Breaths and focus on the present by using your senses to feel, see, smell and hear your surroundings. Look for something beautiful or new. Remember that this practice is building strength, confidence and unshakable peace. Below, list some consistencies in your life where you might have a need to do, fill some silence, distract from some tension, etc. Then describe how you will loosen your grip on these perceived needs using the techniques previously mentioned.

Needs, Shoulds, and Tight Grips List REFRAMED

_____

_____

_____

_____

_____

_____

_____

_____

_____

_____

_____

_____

_____

_____

_____

_____

_____

_____

_____

_____

> "I wasn't leaving my house or driving. I was in complete panic all day and night. I wasn't eating. I lost 70lbs and was running to the ER, it was awful. I talked with khail and it changed my whole perspective. After one call I changed so much. A month later and I am driving by myself! I highly recommend Khail."
> **-Nikki Womack**

Bonus #5: Eliminating Panic Attacks

I know what you're thinking. "Khail, why wouldn't you put this in the beginning? This is my only problem!" As I said, I know what I am doing. If I tell you how to distract yourself from panic without teaching you the tools, rituals and lifestyle changes you need to keep them away forever, it will be no different than taking a benzo or running from your problem.

I am teaching you how to be FREE of panic attacks, not how to hide from them. By following my program, not taking life too seriously, being gentle on and kind to yourself, you are building the foundation necessary to eliminate this garbage once and for all in your life.

Panic attacks will happen along this journey. Keep your eyes on the prize and know that you are doing everything you can to eliminate them. Remind yourself this every time you start asking silly questions like "why". They will be a thing of the past at exactly the right time in your life, whether that takes 2 weeks or 2 years, it is worth it.

In the meantime, to help you eliminate panic attacks, seek presence. Pause Breathe the moment you start to notice symptoms. Gently guide your attention to the positive and begin to use your senses to pull yourself out of your head. What do you see that is beautiful? Name a few things! What can you hear that you're grateful for? What can you smell? Smells are the most powerful as they're directly linked to memory. Try tasting something even if it is just your mouth. Lastly, what do you feel that is good? Sunlight, breeze, strength in your hands?

Lastly, slowly get up, walk away or change the scenery. Don't just sit there and suffer through these. React to them calmly, doing your Pause Breathing, and bring your senses into this!

Try not to hate panic attacks. Try not to dwell in them. Try not to have a tight grip. You're not making any mistakes. It just takes practice. You've got this. I am sending you love.

Practical Solutions for Your *Problems*

"Life has no limitations except for the ones you make."
-Les Brown

If you've made it this far and still cannot relate, I want to provide some more specific examples, but know that your ego is hiding the truth from you. Your answers are here, and you need only consistency and application. But Simba is clever and has put blinders over your eyes. What I mean is that your specific anxiety can be calmed by everything you've read, despite how specific.

If your fear is **driving** or being far from home, the keys lie in presence, focusing your attention on the positive, seeking higher truths, creating a solid foundation and setting small goals. Be present with your surroundings down to the most minute details: the feeling of the steering wheel, the seat, the sounds around you and the smells. When your attention is not on the positive, always interrupt the negative with Pause Breaths and very **calmly** focus back on your destination. If all else fails, go back to your original positive story. Pick a destination with a purpose. Go to a specific store to get something you really want. Set an end goal like a vacation or something really huge and almost unimaginable. Slowly and calmly build towards this! I will elaborate more on driving as an example in the section "Judgment".

Do not allow yourself to tiptoe back and forth between wondering if you will panic and focusing on good. I see this all the time. Constantly looking over your shoulder and asking if anxiety is there. It is, when you beckon it.

Agoraphobia is another common hurdle I've helped many overcome. Needing a safe-zone is a NEED. Believing you are safe in your house is assuming that you have time.

"The trouble is, you think you have time."
-Buddha

We believe we are safe if we hide under the covers, but we are fragile no matter where we are. Life is not guaranteed anywhere except right here and right now. You need to get outside and live! A fantastic tip that has helped my clients suffering from agoraphobia, driving, and many other needless phobias is **setting small goals.** Tell yourself you are going to walk to the end of the block and back after your morning routine. Don't overthink it. Don't make big elaborate plans with bailout options. Keep your phone out of reach. Practice mindfulness and Pause Breaths and achieve your very small goal. Set the bar as low as you would like to. You can stand in the doorway or even by a window. Make the experience calm above everything. Day by day, increase this. Grow. You've got this.

If your **loved ones** seem to trigger your anxiety, the anxiety is keeping you from truly experiencing these gifts of life. Practicing presence with them moment to moment, Pause Breaths before and during your experience with them, and focusing on being grateful for them will help you regain and grow the experience you wish to have. You can always stop. Stop mid-argument or meltdown and breathe. Name 3 things you love about the other person. Think about why you are with this person or what they truly mean to you, without the emotional weight dictating the current bad experience. Work together, even if they (think they) don't have anxiety, do Pause Breaths together, hold each other and look into one another's eyes for a few breaths. Watch the smiles show up. Watch love shine through. Your children will LOVE the Pause Breaths!

If **work** is the cause of your stress, find something positive to think about. Make a friend over a simple topic of interest you share, focus on the paycheck, or visualize things going your way regularly. Remember to always be feeding the good wolf. Also, just like the weight-loss example, make sure you are only feeding your mind the "right" reasons. Don't be afraid to take risks. We only have this one life. Perhaps you should choose a career path that is more spiritually fulfilling. Take your time and don't make any decisions out of fear.

Heath anxiety is very common. How can you relate these lessons to your health anxiety? Are you being practical by affirming your good health with your physician? Are you feeding the good wolf and wiring your mind for positivity? Are you loving yourself? One of my favorite tips is to use every Pause Breath as a time to put your hand over your heart and tell yourself that you love yourself, that you are strong and healthy. Remember how powerful "I am" is. Research reasons why you are healthy. Live in the present and live every moment to the fullest, coming to terms with the preference of enjoying our fragile lives rather than wasting them in worry. Remember how much your health depends on your happiness! And then remember your response-ability.

Depression can be sneaky. Many people suffering from anxiety don't even know they are depressed. This program is designed to show you how to eliminate this as well, so it doesn't matter. When we are depressed, it is hard to see the bright side, the silver lining, and the cup as half full. Remember that our perspectives are shaped by our intentions, and what we pay attention to creates a subconscious intention. So, if your day is spent worrying and fearing, chances are you may get a little depressed at times. You could easily become very depressed, and I want to share some more helpful tips.

First, everything discussed so far will help and easily could be all that you need. Next, an understanding. Most people don't like the word depression, and that's fine. Why label yourself? Why limit yourself at all? Let's focus on the opposite. Energized!

Excited! Curious! Joyous! Accomplished! One of the keys to beating depression is committing to small, easily attainable goals, and slowly pushing yourself every day. Commitment. Small commitment. Smile while you shower. Do one push-up first thing in the morning. Say hi to someone new today. Getting outside a little everyday goes a long way as well. A dose of sunlight and nature are musts! Plenty of research shows that a brisk, 30-minute walk a few days a week can completely eliminate depression. So, get out there and beat this thing! Want a video on depression? I have a 2-part series you must check out!

Part 1: https://youtu.be/mURitQ_BDqQ
Part 2: https://youtu.be/apTG56vaQcs

If you suffer from **social anxiety**, your true problem is actually suffering from a state of selfishness. This doesn't make you a bad person or anything like that. Hear me out. Most of anxiety sufferers are suffering from selfishness. You have too much attention inward. You are focusing so much on your self. Is my hair okay? Am I standing the right way? Did I just make a funny face? Also, your focus is needing recognition, approval and help from the people around you to assure you that everything is okay. Are you hoping they like you or are you actively trying to be yourself? Being genuine is likable. If people don't like you, good! People that do will find you if you just stay true to being you. Trust me. I tried the other way for most of my life.

To combat this, you need to come at everything from a place of love. If you were made of pure love, (which you are) if you approached others with a loving heart, how would that look? How can you brighten their day? How can you make them feel special? What questions could you ask them to show you are genuinely interested in their lives? How can you be the environment that they need to thrive in? Your state of being is powerful! Stay out of your head and put your attention on spreading smiles around you.

What advice could you apply to your current situation despite your current diagnoses? Remember to affirm the person you want to be by saying, "I am", and interrupting uncomfortable patterns with Pause Breaths. Use the space below to describe your thoughts and ideas, along with anything that resonated with you. Your brain is giving you feedback. Writing it out will help you navigate!

Write your thoughts on this section. Important to see your mind work!

_____

_____

_____

_____

_____

_____

_____

_____

It's a process. Be kind to yourself and cultivate patience.

> *I started having anxiety and panic attacks during my third trimester three years ago. I was so worried about my health and hers I wouldn't leave my bed. After she was born I thought things would get better but they just got worse. I started taking medicine for anxiety and it helped at first but not for long. I changed meds a few times, read lots of books, been to therapy, anxiety groups you name it. I stumbled across Khail's page and learned about his story and thought it had to be impossible to have all these problems cured through his program, but after a video call with him I took a shot. 4 weeks later and amazing how much it had truly helped me with my anxiety and panic. I was avoiding all things that had to be done in life and now I'm up and out doing things every day! I'm able to be a better mother to my beautiful daughter and a better wife. I've learned so much about myself and how to change my life.*
> **-Lindsey Holt**

Judgment

"Look at everything as an infant does – absorbing everything, not judging anything, not labeling anyone."
-Sadhguru

Your journey through life is all about self-discovery and self-love. On the other hand, it is about calming, reducing and eliminating fear. Read this next part slowly and follow me through this before I break it down. Right now, whether or not you're consciously aware of it, you are constantly taking in new information through **the filter of your perspective**. Your perspective is controlled and created by your subconscious intention. Your intention is created by the quality of your attention, which is either stuck in a cycle with your subconscious intention OR your attention is in YOUR control as your conscious awareness. But understand that your conscious awareness is limited by fear, guilt, hate, tension or anything else negative. As you shed these, your conscious awareness expands. From the other perspective, your conscious awareness is expanded by love, inspiration and contentment.

To break it down, it is about judgment. As we walk through life, our senses are looking for things to judge. "Thou shalt not judge" is more for our own good than anyone else's, because our journey is all about self-love. Now, judgment doesn't necessarily mean to look at something negative. Judgment is about having a preconceived notion, an assumption, a belief or understanding about something. But the truth is that you are always looking through a biased filter.

I'd like to use **DRIVING** as an example as I've helped many people crush this anxiety. When you're driving, if you focus on bad drivers, the disregard for fellow humans as people don't slow down and allow others to merge, as people cut each other off and muscle their way in, if you see the stop and go, if you feel pressured by the time, if you notice the woman applying mascara, the man texting, all the mistakes, close calls, poor manners, brake checking, tire marks and broken glass, if you're constantly seeing missed opportunities for you to merge or take exits and these upset you, if you're even struggling to find something good to listen to or focus on, you are paying a lot of negative attention to the world around you. You are judging negatively.

Remember that you don't need to have negative thoughts to feel bad. You may not be aware of the attention you're giving the world, or you may be attempting to pay positive attention, but how you *feel* is most important. Your feelings will dictate your overall state of being and make you feel as if there is no other way to view the world. Your feelings set your intention, which makes it very difficult to give the opposite attention to the world around you.

Step back and see how much positive attention you are giving to this world. Are the levels of positive and negative attention equal? Doubtful. We are wired to seek out what's missing, what needs fixing, and what's wrong. Remember caveman Bob and how this system is wired for survival. Naturally, we feel fine when we are in neutral, and don't seek to find more positive. We often only give negative attention to things. So, if you aren't judging your surroundings as beautiful, safe, humane, courteous, silly, helpful, interesting, curious, or perfectly harmonious, your scale is tilted in the wrong direction.

Note: I know it sounds ridiculous to say that something like Los Angeles traffic, the state of the world, politics or many other things are perfectly harmonious, but if you could stand inside your bloodstream and watch your blood cells tumbling over each other without any sign of a smooth pattern, you may think that was chaotic too. Yet here you are, all perfectly oxygenated.

So, your scale is tipped into the negative. Negativity translates to fear and the weight of that fear is determined by the frequency and weight of the negative information being absorbed. Enough negative attention and now you have an intention to find more. It gets easier. Day by day, year after year you get better and better at seeing the negative and now your intention comes with emotional weight. It might sound like "I just don't like it", "I hate it", or "I can't stand it."

Now your perspective, your opinions and beliefs on driving on the freeway are rooted in this fear all because it is consistently being fueled by your conscious and subconscious judgment of the environment. You begin to attribute triggers to different happenings on the road such as loud noises, inclement weather, or busy traffic. Your "understanding" of this environment is so deeply rooted in emotion, years of negative attention, and a narrow perspective of reality.

Fear becomes the intention through negative judgment.

The truth is that you are limitless. Everything you don't like is an opportunity for your growth. Hate may be a prison, but love is your salvation. The truth is, you need to try to love the freeway. You need to try to love every bit of your journey because through love you will grow and see a bigger picture. Through love, you will gain wisdom. But you don't start with love! You've got to take things slow with this relationship because you haven't trusted the freeway for a long time. You will want to better get to know your fear and start to see it in a different light. Then, maybe someday you and the freeway can have hundreds of little exits together.

All joking aside, there's truth to this. How do you see the freeway in a different light? How can you love the news, the state of affairs, or a person that brought you pain? Look for it! But before you do, you want to create a ritual to ramp up your positivity before you even attempt this task. Train yourself to grab your keys confidently, to walk to your car with eagerness and excitement. Have fun every time you start that engine. Crank up your favorite song and take 5 minutes to get silly. Rev the engine and really overdo your enthusiasm for this trip. Laugh. Laugh out loud, get physical, and feel amazing before you head out. Remember that your emotional state is within your power. **See the Over-the-Top Silliness Ritual in Bonus #1.**

Once you've created a pre-driving ritual, you're ready to hit the road with a great attitude and intention! Keep it up. If you are going to trust the freeway, you'll want to start treating all driving experiences with love, excitement, feelings of freedom and peace, and a sense of control. All driving experiences. So that means no more allowing yourself to feel rushed, no more road rage, no more needs for distraction! Remember "Need versus Want." You take charge of your state of being!

You want to be in control. It is where your anxiety comes from. But you can't control the outcomes of the journey. Truth is, you can't control the outcome of anything. There is not one thing in your life that you are in full control of except for your attention, and then what you do with it. Your state of being is what you truly wish to control. You want to handle danger with cunning and intelligence. You want to handle disaster with gentleness and tact. This is control.

The moment you put your car into drive, take the wheel of your experience by aiming your attention towards higher truth, the reality that serves you. Find the good around you. Every time your mind trails off or you catch yourself saying something like "check out this *&^%$#@!", calmly shift your attention back to feeding the good wolf. Forgive them, know they're innocent, look for something they do well and recognize when you've been guilty of something similar in the past. As perfect of a driver as you may be, we all make little random mistakes and we've all been lucky.

Breathe slowly and deeply along your journey. Look for things to love in your car and all around you. The car is now your mental gym. How many reps will you do on your next drive? If you normally see 10 things wrong with the world around you while driving, try to find 100 things that are right. If you normally try to avoid thinking about it at all and you are simply feeling about it poorly, how often are you uncomfortable? If you only begin to feel anxiety towards the end of the trip, you will want to make sure you are feeling great well before that, see it coming, and continue to practice your focused attention on the good.

If you aren't actively creating a positive space, your neutrality will eventually lead back to negative. You have old wiring in there. Don't take breaks from this mental gym. This is your dojo. This is where you will transform. Your entire life will get significantly better by eliminating this one fear.

Remember, it takes time. It is a process. After enough practice with your attention, your focus muscle will become resilient against seeing the bad. Your ability to see good will get easier. Your ability to feel good will get easier. Your perspective will loosen and shift towards safety, enjoyment, and ease. And you will arrive at your destination without fear. This will be a thing of the past. Stay consistent. You've got this.

How can I unravel my fears, and create a plan using this chapter?

_____

_____

_____

_____

_____

_____

_____

_____

_____

_____

_____

_____

_____

_____

_____

_____

> *"For the last 10 years I haven't been able to drive more than a 5-mile radius because of anxiety. It was crippling. I had these unrealistic fears of pending doom and haven't even gone to the grocery store myself in years!! But after just a few conversations with Khail, I am getting my life back. For the first time in at least 10 years I went shopping all by myself. And it was empowering! It felt amazing! Just last night I drove 20 minutes away after dark, in the rain, by myself! There's no stopping me now I'm breaking the chains of anxiety!"*
> **-Laura Tabor**

Depersonalization, Derealization and Consciousness

When you label me, you rob me of who I could be.

Have you ever experienced detachment from reality, a sort of out of mind experience where you lose your sense of self or your ability to understand and label your surroundings? This inability to label something like a chair often strikes fear into people suffering from anxiety. And for understandable reasons. But not for the reasons most people think. This is more like waking up from a dream only to realize you actually are flying, realizing you have no idea how to fly. I'll explain.

Anxiety is a constant inward focus towards bodily feelings, emotions and thoughts. I refer to anxiety as "absent-mindfulness", because it is the exact skill you need to start beating anxiety, absent of the control.

A **label** is a title given to something based on a judgment which is an opinion, a biased opinion disguising itself as knowledge. For instance, when you see a tree, it isn't just the label of the tree that you see but your understanding of this giant object as a plant, and your understanding of plants. And it might stop there! But judgments are biased opinions disguising themselves as knowledge. So, there could be emotional weight based on a memory or countless other predispositions towards what a tree is. One could see a tree and see a forest on every extension of each branch, considering that each seed has the potential to grow a forest. But whether these judgments are true or limited is irrelevant. While we are playing scientist looking at the tree, the tree is being. It is growing at a very slow rate, digesting sunlight, feeling the wind with every leaf and twig.

To experience the tree fully (or any object or situation) the predispositions, judgments, labels, and assumptions need to be removed. After seeing all these details about a tree, imagine laying eyes on this magical forest creator for the first time in your life, but with the wisdom you currently have and an anxiety-free, very full heart. See how labels rob the experience?

Maybe trees aren't your thing. Imagine your children, your partner, your pets. Imagine seeing these beautiful things without carrying ANY subconscious "knowledge" about who they are. Imagine, seeing your spouse with fresh eyes, without knowing what she's thinking or without feeling all the past fights. Imagine looking at your child without feeling agitated or exhausted. Imagine seeing nature as if you have never opened your eyes before.

Labels and judgments filter your experience.

To be depersonalized is to experience life anew, to experience through the eyes of the higher-self, the real you, the you without the baggage, without the trauma or the pain, the limitless version of human consciousness. Derealization is a taste of enlightenment. And when you learn how to wield mindfulness for calm and confidence, you start to tap into these vibrant and curious states of presence, and you learn how to shed everything about you and your life that doesn't serve you.

Do not be afraid to see without labels for I believe that it is a taste of the highest levels of human consciousness. Embrace it.

> *"Panic attacks cost me my job, my apartment, my life. I couldn't be around crowds. I didn't want to be on medication again. Then I found Khail. I literally cried after watching his first video. I knew that I knew that I KNEW this was where I would learn how to beat this! After just the first week I was 90% calmer! Now, if anxiety tries to rear its ugly head, I beat it down with techniques Khail taught me. I have learned from Khail and highly recommend him to anyone who is suffering."*
> **-Sue Wagner**

Forgiveness

"He who is devoid of the power to forgive is devoid
of the power to love."
-Dr. Martin Luther King Jr.

To forgive means to let go of the pain. To carry a grudge is like sipping poison in hopes that someone else will die or holding a hot ember with the intention to throw it at an enemy. One person is definitely suffering in these scenarios.

Remember how the subconscious mind works? Remember the orange story? This hate, pain, sadness or whatever you are carrying is poisoning you. It is creating an intention in your life to seek more. An intention to seek more pain, more relationships with trust issues, more abuse, more fear. This intention creates action towards the very thing you're trying to avoid in the form of attention, thoughts, feelings, reactions and plenty more. You will have what is called a "self-fulfilling prophecy". You will inadvertently attract more of what you hate by hanging onto the pain of the past.

Forgiveness is not about condoning a behavior. It isn't about blindly trusting someone again. So, **don't think you owe anyone anything** or that you have to go back to a toxic environment. Forgiveness is about letting go of that hot ember and being happy. It is about allowing yourself to grow and experience from a loving set of eyes. It is an act of self-love, and loving yourself, improving your well-being, is the greatest gift you can give the world. If you are currently in an abusive relationship, get out. But if the only abuse is your thoughts against you, it is time to dive in.

"Darkness cannot drive out darkness; only light can do that. Hate
cannot drive out hate; only love can do that."
-Dr. Martin Luther King Jr.

Just like fighting anxiety with calm, you must fight the hate in your heart with love. You must love yourself enough to want your own happiness above everything else!

To take it a step further, take a mindful step back from everything in your life. How did you get here? If you're following along for weeks in this journey, the way this is designed, how do you feel now? Meaning, if you feel stronger now, more than ever before, or you believe this journey will make you better than ever, can you adopt a perspective that makes the past seem worth it? Can you see how the pain has placed you on a path for greatness? Can you imagine that your enemies taught you lessons, and that pain has been your greatest teacher?

If you know you will be happier, more grateful, a better spouse, parent, friend, if you know your life will be richer than the average persons with love and presence, how did you get here? Could you lower your guard enough at this point to be truly grateful for every wrong turn you've taken, every bump in the road, every traumatic experience and all the suffering you've carried and endured, knowing that it set you on a course to greater peace and richer happiness?

Taking forgiveness to the level of gratitude can bring you a sense of appreciation for the masterpiece that is your life. The culmination of bringing every moment together to this very instant where you decide to let go of pain and suffering and embrace everything that will come your way with a fresh and open heart, with a mindset for growth, and with an attitude that says, "what am I going to learn next?"

This idea may not be for everyone. If it doesn't sit right with you, I don't want you to forget it. Come back to it after a few weeks of mindful Pause Breathing and healthy routines. Imagine what this new perspective could do for your life before you immediately say that forgiveness isn't for you.

Imagine the positive ripple effect you will have on the rest of the world when you let go of the suffering you're carrying!

When I was a toddler, my mother started "disciplining" with a wooden paddle. She inscribed the words "KHAIL'S CURE" on the spanking device and would regularly use it. The paddle wasn't the only way she abused young Khail, but it serves a good point for this section. Through the years of mental and physical abuse I developed a ton of issues that ultimately added up to the suicidal and very lost Khail I described at the beginning of this book. But as you've read, not only did I turn my life around, but I put myself on an incredibly strong and happy path, and I've helped SO MANY do the same! I never would have had the abilities, the drive, the passion, or any of the skills to do what I do had my mother not been in the state she was in. Truth. You may argue that I didn't *need* to experience the trauma to get to where I am. Perhaps.

Wisdom is not given but gathered along the journey.

Without the experience, how could I relate? Without the experience, how could I know with conviction that you will get better? Without my past, why would you even listen? See, mom didn't raise me the way I wanted her to, but she did do the best she could with the tools she was using. She wasn't waking up each day reading books like these. She was waking up in fear and frustration. She carried years of her own negative experiences into our lives together. The meaning may have had different intentions, but when she wrote "KHAIL'S CURE" on that paddle, I know she didn't have a clue as to just how right she was.

I am grateful for my trials, for they have pushed me to peace.

What haven't you let go of? What forgiveness could take place in your life? How would your life change if you could put down the past? Better yet, how would your life change if you saw purpose in your pain? How could this affect others? In the space below take some time to answer these questions for yourself.

_____

_____

_____

_____

_____

_____

_____

_____

_____

_____

_____

_____

_____

_____

_____

_____

_____

_____

_____

_____

_____

_____

Sometimes the understanding of forgiveness and weeks of the foundational work don't provide enough relief. Don't worry. Keep up with feeding the good wolf and time will help. That means continuously reframing your thoughts to elicit good feelings. You may also want to try a deeper exercise. One of my favorites I have my clients do is write EVERYTHING out. Let's say you also had an abusive parent. Take as much time as you need to write about the pain, experiences, expectations, damages, and anything else. Once you've finished, describe why you want to forgive them. Something along the lines of "I am ready to be happy" will do just fine, but make it your own words. Lastly, tear it up or burn it. This physical and dramatic experience has amazing neurological effects and has helped so many people. You are physically letting go of it all.

Ultimately, your peace is the most important goal to strive for.

> *"It hasn't even been a month since I contacted Khail to help me with my anxiety and I'm already seeing BIG changes. It's like I'm seeing the world with a brandnew set of eyes thanks to him. I'm calmer, happier, and most importantly so very grateful for this beautiful life I'm living. He has this infectious energy that just instantly puts me at ease. It's hard to explain so I ask you to contact him and feel it for yourself. You deserve it! Thank you Khail. I can't wait to see what a year from now looks like."*
> **-Jacky Hong**

Gratitude

"When you are grateful, fear disappears, and abundance appears."
-Tony Robbins

Whether you thank god, the universe or simply yourself, see the good in your environment and truly pause for a moment to appreciate it. Being grateful takes practicing presence and crushing anxiety to another level!

Gratitude is a mental-illness eliminator. It wires the mind for heightened states of bliss and inspiration. Researchers at Berkley believe that practicing gratitude rewires the mind for more positivity in just four weeks, and it even elicits feelings of compassion for others and feelings of belonging to the rest of the world. This sense of belonging to something bigger than us is the remedy for the void that so many experience.

It is said that it is impossible to be in a state of fear, negativity, or apathy while practicing gratitude. The fastest way to experience more of these beautiful feelings is to change your positive thoughts after each conscious Pause Breaths to a thought of gratitude. The **key** that most people miss with gratitude is the feeling. We are all grateful for our kids, our jobs, a safe place to live, air, water, etc., right? No. **Gratitude is a state of being.** It isn't an idea. Usually when we say we are grateful, we only mean it with our minds and not with our hearts. This honesty doesn't make you a bad person. It shows consideration. We want to be in a state of gratitude for these things, so we had better get real with them.

To get from an idea to a feeling, start with as many reasons, thoughts, memories, and understandings about this idea that you can imagine. If you want to be grateful for your house for example, list everything you love about it, describe the memories you've experienced, what it means to you and your family, and use your understanding of what having a house means to begin to create an environment to manifest gratitude. Next, describe the kinds of feelings these thoughts elicit and the feelings you would like to experience. You may write that having a house gives you security, pride, and admiration for your hard work. Next, think about some actions you can do to experience gratitude. You may change your Pause Breaths to think about your house. You can stop and admire your surroundings from time to time. You will want to avoid anything negative about the house or use opportunities like a sink breaking to give yourself a gratitude reality check by saying "I am blessed to have a great sink to fix. I love that I can take care of the things I love." Put your gratitude into practice! For reference, go back to Figures 4A and 4B, and use the imagery to map out your gratitude plan.

In the space below, using the information above and Figures 4a and 4b, write out an example for yourself on how to be grateful for something important to you

_____

_____

_____

_____

_____

_____

_____

As an amazing practice, every morning and every evening, start to log something or a few things you are grateful for. Remember that you want to truly FEEL them. Don't be too repetitive as you do this and devote a few minutes to sitting and breathing with that feeling of gratitude. **Allowing these habits to feel stale will have adverse effects**, but if you devote time, energy and attention, you will feel the effects VERY quickly. Writing in the morning sets a positive intention to experience more things to be grateful for throughout the day. Writing in the evening is great because this is usually the time where we are most ungrateful. It will help you set your intention for your subconscious before drifting off to sleep and can dramatically improve your sleep quality. If you find that this practice is getting stale, get back to trying to FEEL good about it. This routine can change everything about your life. As with everything you've learned so far, it takes practice. Practice is meditation. Throughout your day, meditating on a state of gratitude means seeking to feel grateful as often as you remember to.

> *"I haven't had a panic attack in 4 months since Khail's coaching. I was desperate when we first connected and since then he's taught me so much. I couldn't even breathe properly and now I overcome panic attacks! My sleep, exercise, health and everything I was triggered by has gotten so much better. I can even control my thoughts much better! I thank God for Khail."*
> **-Alma Marisol**

Meditation

"What we fear most is usually what we most need to do."
-Tim Ferriss

Something that has helped me stay on this path through poverty, homelessness, sickness and loss is my ability to calm my thoughts and get into the present moment. But I am no expert at sitting still or being quiet for long. In fact, I know many who were experts at these things, yet they continued to struggle with anxiety before my help.

Meditation is better practiced constantly throughout the day rather than a morning or evening ritual.

That's not to say that deep meditations and learning to sit still for a long time doesn't have its benefits! Perhaps for another book. This is to teach you to eliminate anxiety, not to astral project. Meditation is simply a focused practice. When you are consciously breathing throughout the day, you're meditating. You're meditating when you choose to feed the good wolf, rather than getting into a negative conversation. You're meditating when you decide that your uncomfortable state doesn't need a reason, and you choose to create a positive state of being with your thoughts. You're meditating when you pause to reflect and feel good about yourself.

So, I do recommend that you take some time every morning and every night to do a simple meditation. But I urge you to meditate on your ideal self 24/7/365 for the rest of your life! Practicing mindfulness and constantly sharpening your art of peace will be tremendously rewarding for your life and those around you.

There is no right way to meditate, but there are some wrong ways. Don't meditate with an expectation to get anything out of it. Don't meditate forcefully. If you're trying to quiet your mind, remember to always do it calmly.

When I was incredibly anxious, and my mind was constantly racing, I devised a way to meditate and I'll now describe that for you. First, aim very low. If you can't sit still for one minute, start meditating by sitting still for 30 seconds.

The last thing you want to do is relate this calming experience to something that causes you stress.

Next, eventually you want to get to a place where you feel very quieted, calmed and blissful. But to go from anxiety to this state takes focus. I've found that counting your breaths can be very helpful in developing this focus. But even counting doesn't ensure focus, so you may want to really spam up your minds bandwidth by counting. For example, when inhaling, you can silently count 1-1-1-1-1-1-1, exhale: 2-2-2-2-2-2-2 and so on. The key here is to practice focus by using your mind consciously for extended periods of time. It may start with a millisecond, but it will grow.

Setting an intention before you sit quietly is also helpful. After you gain a little comfort in meditating, you will be able to see your mind work for you, delivering ideas that reflect your intention.

Stay consistent. Like everything else you've learned from this program, meditation is like learning an instrument. You're playing the mind. Master it and you master everything.

Lastly, always remember not to take this, or anything in life too seriously.

> *"I have been dealing with anxiety for a little over 2 years now. Having panic attacks pretty much every day. My anxiety had gotten very bad to the point I was terrified of leaving my house and just felt like I was going to die at any moment. Once I started Khail's program, everything changed for the better. I am now able to shut everything off and focus on getting myself to a calm state. I am a happier and more positive person. I am facing my fears and love the path that I am on!"*
> **-Keyri Velasquez**

The Beginning

"Before enlightenment, chop wood, carry water. After enlightenment, chop wood, carry water."
-Zen Saying

Yes, you've read the title to the last section correctly. This is not the end, but the beginning. Every single moment you are bringing yourself into the present is the beginning. Every moment is an opportunity to understand deeper, to experience richer and to love harder. Every moment is new. Your understanding of your current-self will pale in comparison to the shining star you are growing to become. Your state of consciousness in this moment may *understand* that this is all that you are, and knows that new skills will be learned, but it will be this current version of you that will learn them. The truth is that your current state of conscious awareness has many deeper layers.

What you know now, you can know richer tomorrow. As you reflect on your progress, using your **Brag Book**, and review your favorite lessons, you will see this richer awareness take shape. Words you once understood will begin to take on a deeper meaning. It feels like **waking up**. Keep climbing! With each new layer of conscious awareness comes a broader experience, a wider lens through which you will view the world, a greater understanding for any and all, and a more useful toolbelt!

Life will continue to throw you curve balls, but you must know that you are the greatest batter for the job, that you always have everything you need to take on any and all of life's challenges. Know that wisdom comes from the journey. Don't be afraid to ask questions.

Never fear being wrong, for if you can definitively know you're wrong, the correct path will be much clearer.

My favorite saying to carry with me through every experience is "**Everything is happening FOR me**". It may seem a little egotistical, but if you look at a problem as a stepping stone, if you look at a negative feeling as an indicator for direction or improvement, and if you see life as a perpetual opportunity game, you will continue to grow until the day you trade your body in for a different experience.

As I mentioned in the beginning of this book, I chose this path. It has continued to deliver experience and wisdom. I couldn't be happier living out of a backpack for months, sleeping in a car, waking up every day not knowing how I was going to eat, and spending 12 hour a day in coffee shops using Wi-Fi to reach people all over the world.

Just a few days ago, the car I'd been living in for 2 months was rear-ended by a sweet young woman who didn't notice traffic was stopped on the freeway. The car is totaled.

Insurance will cover it, but it will only pay for what we owed. I don't know what I will do next, but I am going home and I believe everything will work out. Things always seem to, despite how we feel when we are knee deep in the mud. I do know that I am blessed to have walked away with minimal soreness and bruising. I do know that we are lucky she hit me and nobody else, because I am alive, well, and have no interest in suing her (despite our debt and other circumstances, and living in the suing capital of the US). I do know that hugging her, assuring her that she doesn't have to feel bad and bringing her to tears that night was a powerfully loving experience for both of us. And considering I help people with driving phobias, I have such a rich, firsthand experience to now offer even better help.

If you couldn't tell, I tried to give it all in this book. What I do with coaching is something more that flows through me, but everything starts with these principals and tactics I've squeezed into this book. Don't be afraid to read things a few times. Don't be afraid to reach out to my community and continue your growth. This is your life! Make it yours!

I am writing this from a place without suffering. I no longer struggle with anxiety or any mental illness, suffer from worry, fear or anything else. I experience pain, doubt, flares of discomfort, but I address, assess and grow through these. It is my intention to learn how to grow even happier, more present and grateful, and to continue to help others along their journey towards enlightenment and inner-peace. I want to heal you and anyone else that wants the healing, and I know that whatever this does and I do comes from within you, just as my gifts come from within me. I AM HUMAN, and so are you. My mission is to help create a world without suffering, a more unified and value-conscious world. I will relieve hundreds of millions from anxiety, depression and more, and it is apparent that nothing will stop me.

I love you. Thank you for reading this. May you always get exactly what you need and never lose sight of what truly matters in your life. To your serenity.

-Khail Kapp

Professional Super Hero

Helpful Resources

Your FREE Cheat-Sheet: https://khailkapp.com/cheat-sheet
Free 1-mo Access to Course/Community ($10/mo after):https://goo.gl/xvj1bM
Coaching and Speaking Opportunities: https://khailkapp.com/
Connect with me on Facebook: https://facebook.com/khail.kapp/
Subscribe on YouTube: https://youtube.com/khaikapp/
Join the Free Community: https://facebook.com/groups/khail.kapp/
Donate to Khail: https://PayPal.me/khailkapp

Made in the USA
Middletown, DE
30 December 2018